Praise for **PAREN**

MW00586127

"I have known Phil Harmon the fact that he is a "family man" and that he has demonstrated an intentional, proactive, and positive approach to loving and mentoring his children, grandchildren and great-grandchildren throughout the highs and lows of life. In this book, he takes fifty years of parenting experience and shares how all of us can be the parents and grandparents we want to be. His practical suggestions on how to develop close family ties and nurture those relationships long-term make this book a great and important read."

—**Denny Rydberg,** President, Young Life

"This is timely advice from a man who is tenacious about his love for his family."

—**Drs. Les and Leslie Parrott**, Authors of
The Parent You Want to Be

"We have had many gatherings with Phil and Esther and their growing, glowing clan. What an amazing example of what can happen regardless of tough times, when faith and love make up the center of family. This is a fun read and the ideas are infectious....we know from personal experience!"

—**Treena and Graham Kerr,** Co-creators of
The Galloping Gourmet TV Series

"*Parenting Lasts a Lifetime* is an enjoyable collection of stories and useful tips for all stages of parenting. I look forward to putting them into practice!"

—**Josh Kelley**, Author of *Radically Normal*
(Harvest House, July 2014)

"I have never met a man who is more dedicated to his family than Phil, and he has done us all a wonderful service by describing his family experiences in this book."

—**J. Alan Cook**, MD, Psychiatrist

"I have known Phil and his family for 39 years and I will attest to what a dynamic family system they have. Their faith has guided them through the most difficult times of life. They are real and transparent about the good the bad and the ugly parts of real life. I gladly give my endorsement and encourage you to read *Parenting Lasts a Lifetime*. The title alone calls for attention, and the pages within reveal wisdom needed to guide all future generations."

—**Edward Nixon**, Author of *The Nixons: A Family Portrait*

"This book is packed with fun ways to get serious about building family integrity and bridging the inevitable generational gap, humorously told by a family-man who has experienced some of the utmost ups and deepest downs life has to offer."

—**Bruce Wersen**, Senior Pastor
His Place Church, Burlington, WA

"Phil Harmon is a fun-loving, creative and determined guy. I know. I met him during a very difficult time in both our lives. I watched him apply the parenting principles he writes about in the most challenging situation possible. He persevered and did it well. Read this book, apply its principles and you'll be a better parent and person for it."

—**Cliff Tadema**, Senior Pastor
Christ the King Community Church
Mount Vernon, WA

Parenting Lasts a Lifetime

Phil Harmon

Jacqueline Rae

All scripture quotations are taken from the HOLY BIBLE: NEW INTERNATIONAL VERSION®. © 1973, 1978, 1984 by International Bible Society.

Printed in the United States of America

Dickinson Press, Inc.

Diane Johnson, Chief Editor and Layout Editor

Melissa Goodhead, Editor

Lisa Anderson, Cover Design

Amy Mason, Cover Concept

"...teach them to your children,
talking about them when you sit at home
and when you walk along the road, when you
lie down and when you get up."
~ Deuteronomy 11:19

Table of Contents

Dedicated to the two mothers of my children. Your love and support have made parenting and grandparenting a joy and an adventure.

Esther Harmon

Velda Harmon, 1934 to 1986

Forward

I love the Harmon family. I've seen them go through many seasons—ups and downs—and one thing is certain: they prize family life. Phil and his wife Esther are wholehearted parents and grandparents who won't let anything get in the way of building stronger family connections.

One of my favorite memories with Phil happened several years ago when he and my dad hosted a Father Son Weekend at Camp Harmony. Dad and I were each asked to speak at this event where the main point was the importance of passing the baton from one generation to the next with faith and high expectation to continue a strong family legacy. Phil doesn't cut corners when he is trying to make a point. He purchased relay runner batons for each of the fathers and held a closing ceremony where each father pressed the baton into the hand of his son to symbolically urge him to continue the race of family leadership.

We always enjoy visits with Phil and his family because I get to hear about all the fun and zany things they have done together. This man has a treasure trove of ideas to build family relationship. Who thinks of some of these things? Phil is not the kind of guy who simply takes his family out to dinner. He will take them out to dinner and ask to be seated in the wine cellar and have the proprietor tell them all about the history of the restaurant. How creative is that?

Phil loves being a parent and grandparent and he leads by example with a true zeal for life, relationships and faith in God. I have witnessed their family dynamic and have seen the benefits of the fun way they approach life. This purposeful way of living has strengthened this family and now these attributes are being handed down from generation to generation.

There are many nuggets of gold in the pages of this book and I am very glad my friend Phil took the time to write them out, so we could all benefit from them.

Les Parrott, Ph.D.
Author of *You're Stronger Than You Think*
LesAndLeslie.com

Taking Responsibility

The problem with writing a book is that you feel like everything you write has to be fulfilled in your own life. A parenting book seems to be an especially tricky undertaking as you must measure up to your own "good advice." There is no such thing as perfect parenting, and many of us will find it to be downright messy at times. One of my goals in writing this book is to show how you can have a positive parenting experience through the good, the bad, and the ugly of family life.

It hasn't always been easy to put the ideas in this book into practice. As every parent can attest, we do our best, but life has enough blind-siding curves to keep us all humble. The intent of this book is to reach out to parents who are wondering how to strengthen and deepen their family involvement. It is also meant to encourage anyone who has made a life-changing blunder; your parenting role is still important, so don't give up! It is not about the mistakes you make along the journey. It is about taking responsibility and finishing well.

Does this stuff work when life throws you a curve? Yes, it does. It works through the normal everyday challenges, and I will attest it works when tough stuff finds you later in life.

These principles, lived out during the first thirty years of my parenting journey, carried our family through the death of my first wife, and they stood the test of adversity during a period of time when I was incarcerated in federal prison camp for securities violations. As a family, our world was shaken to the core during these times. Many would have understood if there had been splits in the family or even divorce. However, none of that came to pass. As a family, we all made a decision to stick to our principles, to be guided by our faith, and to work through the pain together.

A personal setback does not eliminate you from your family role, and it is not the sum total of who you are*. If this is you, turn your personal setback into a growth experience and make a comeback!

Confinement in a low-security federal prison camp gave me a lot of focused time to ponder my values, study, and develop into the person who penned these thoughts. I worked through issues of pride and control which were very high mountains to climb as I took responsibility for my wrongdoings and the people my actions had affected. Even while incarcerated, I applied these parenting principles the best I could through phone calls, letters, visitations, and by writing lists of things I planned to do with my family once I returned.

It doesn't matter whether your setback was monumental, slight, or simply the neglect of responsibilities you know you should have taken on. Today is the day to hit the "re-start" button and communicate authentically and honestly with your family. Say to yourself, "I am taking responsibility."

*Clearly, this statement is meant for people who are not dangerous or threatening to family members.

Introduction

Begin Right Where You Are

It doesn't really matter when you start or where. Just start! Be proactive about establishing a strong family. Even if you are the Lone Ranger in your family, yell, "Hi-ho, Silver!" and make this your aim.

This book is not intended to flood you with an overwhelming list of seemingly unattainable ideas. First read through the entire book and just enjoy the stories to get the big picture. Then go back through the book, choose a couple ideas that appeal to you, and apply them to your family. Then go onto another and another, until you have developed a cache of family objectives, traditions, memories, and habits that are formed around your love for one another.

We have to start where we are in life. If you have young children, fantastic! You can get going with a plan and raise them with exciting adventures, developing a distinct family culture that is all your own. If you are older, even much older, or your family is fragmented due to unfortunate circumstances or geographical separation, it shouldn't stop you. Today is the day for you to make that meaningful investment in your family.

Mother Teresa of Calcutta had a great way of getting people focused. When asked what a person can do to help the world, she would say, "You just need to do the thing that's in front of you." Take a couple ideas from this book and apply them to your family, then look and listen. Don't miss it! You will start to see a spirit of life, love, communication, and bonding forming within your family. It takes time, clear objectives, and intentional practice, but the sooner you start the sooner you will enjoy the results.

Keep chipping away at this plan and if you struggle, get right back on track. This is a journey with great adventures along the way, but all road trips have their blowouts. Just find your spare tire, blow new air into it, and get back on the journey. Your family is worth it!

"I Do"

Do you, Phil, take Esther, her children and future grandchildren, to love and cherish and to be your very own?"

The seaside patio of our Camano Island home was our chapel. Other than immediate family, the only guests were seagulls soaring nearby. The decorations were subtle, but the excitement of the day trembled in the air. This was a personal moment and the newness of the autumn air following a hot summer impressed me with the promise of this new season of our lives together.

"I do."

Esther answered, "I do," to the same question, and we have been "doing" ever since. My life is blessed because of her active devotion to those two words.

"I do" is one of the smallest sentences in the world and yet it carries more weight, more promise, and more conviction than any other. "I do" has given us a lively, adventurous, growing marriage because we spend our time planning and building together for the future and for a full life. We work side by side to carry out the promise we made to each other and our combined family.

I love the idea of life being a continual exercise in learning, growing, and stretching. It was a second marriage for both of us and when Esther and I said "I do," it was a promise to spend the second half of our lives *doing* as much as we could with the purpose of building a strong family.

Esther had been acquainted with my family for years before we were married; she had catered several dinner parties for my first wife Velda, to whom I was married for thirty-one years before her passing on Thanksgiving Day 1986.

Esther didn't marry me, she married my family. She was attracted to the magnetic spirit that was alive at all our gatherings. The jovial atmosphere of dinner party laughter would carry from the dining room to the kitchen as she overheard the positive tone of the after-dinner chatter and banter. We are a family that displays affection and closeness, and all of our gatherings are filled with joy and laughter. Oh, we certainly have our own disasters and small dysfunctions, but at the heart of our clan, a spirit of closeness and joy is our norm.

Being honest, neither of these women was as attracted to me as they were to my family. Velda was my high school sweetheart and spent a lot of time in our family home where my parents poured out words of encouragement and support to everyone they met. Friends would remark about how much fun my parents were and snickered when they never missed an opportunity to give each other a flirtatious squeeze or a peck on the lips right in front of us. Outward displays of love and words of affirmation filled our lives, giving our family and friends a strong sense of security and acceptance.

During WWII, our family lived in the shabbiest house on the block, a literal tarpaper shack located behind the greenhouse my father owned. The lackluster appearance of our house was no deterrent; this was the house where everyone wanted to spend time, because spending time in our home meant spending time in the warmth of my parents' welcoming spirit.

My parents invested time in people. They didn't just allow my siblings and me to have friends over to hang out; they would engage all of us, coaxing us into playing games with them. At first we might refuse the offer, acting as if it was of no interest, but my folks were not easily put off. They would bring out games like Sorry, Rook, or Yahtzee and get all of us playing. Before long we were all laughing and relating to one another over rich conversation, leaving everyone feeling special and welcomed.

Evenings were often spent with my dad on the floor shooting marbles and wrestling with my brother and me. One of our favorite pastimes was when dad would bring home a giant cardboard paper roll from the flower shop and we would have contests to see how long we could balance on top of it or how far we could roll without falling off. Mom would fill our stomachs with an evening snack and fill our hearts with the way she supported all of us.

We didn't have a lot of money, but we had deep wealth; a wealth of love and a family spirit that was modeled for me daily. I wanted to see this tone and family culture continued, even refined, in my own family.

Building Family Relationships

Building a stouthearted family spirit means being intentional in the way we connect with all members of the family. By creating enticing gatherings filled with love, acceptance and carefree activities, we give everyone a desire to come together and a foundation to build strong relationships. The younger grandchildren love being a part of such a big family and the older ones have grown to value the reliable relationships.

Whether it is through one-on-one time with a child, or a larger gathering with multiple activities, we are able to make deposits into their lives and grow our relationships with each one.

By modeling virtues that we want to see lived out in our children and grand-children, we invite them to engage with one another, learn new things, and develop the assurance of strong roots that link them to a great past, and strong wings which will carry them to an exciting future.

Together, my wife and I share the goal of being enthusiastically present in the lives of our children and grandchildren. We attempt to impress upon them that people are more important than things and we set out to prove that by our actions. Kids of all ages will refuse the best offer made to them if they feel it is a mandate. We are so glad when they show up at our house or for family events, but we understand that they have demands on their lives that will keep them from always being able to attend.

One of the greatest rewards of being a well-connected family is seeing our children developing healthy relationships in all directions, including with their spouse's family. We understand that these younger married couples and families just can't be everywhere. We always endeavor to show our children and grandchildren our great desire to have them present at our gatherings, but we never ever want to make them feel guilty if they can't come.

These principles weren't techniques or methods with a lot of research behind them. No, this was a gut feeling about what we needed to do to build family harmony, and we pray this will

Family Legacy

A legacy is a way of living that is started in one generation and continues beyond that generation's lifespan. This is a vision and tradition that is cast, executed and continued beyond you because it has brought so much value to your family. It is a rich inheritance that is passed from generation to generation.

repeat through our future generations and become our family legacy.

Strive for a Unique Family Culture

Someone can hand you a promising list containing fifty points to carry out in order to have a healthy marriage and family life. If you carry out every point exactly, but lack the right intent, it will not benefit the relationship. It's a fraud. The only reason for carrying out the principles in this book is because you genuinely care to deepen the relationship among individuals in your family. Who cares about appearances? Meaningful actions that lead to deepening relationships are indisputable.

The worthy goal is to create a unique family culture that inspires each person to grab hold and invest in the common vision. It sets in motion a tradition of replicating this system up and down the generations. Younger family members have a freshness and zeal for life and new ideas about innovation and technology that greatly benefit the older folks; the older generation pours insight and experience into the generations that come after. It is a beautifully symbiotic connection.

Having an effective family with an "us" way of life brings substance and energy to the ordinary day-to-day routine. Like you, we want to be a family that relates well to each other, both up and down the generations, and to demonstrate a love for being together. We want to establish an atmosphere of quality time spent together where the vibes are good and every member feels accepted and valued. A well-connected family is possible for anyone who is genuinely willing to invest time and energy to reach this worthy goal.

Anchor Points

Start a list
Don't just think this through; actually write out the things you really value about your family. Think about those aspects and let others know what you value about them. Include in your list a number of things *your* parents did right.

Describe Your Job
As you consider your calling as a parent, how do you define your job description?

Evaluate
Work to gain a solid understanding of the current state of health and happiness for your family. To help with your assessment, consider the following questions:

- Is your family communicating openly?
- Does everyone know how each family member gives and receives love? According to Gary Chapman, in his book, *The Five Love Languages,* everyone gives and receives love through one of these five avenues: Physical touch, words of affirmation, gifts, acts of service, or quality time spent together.
- Are you holding family meetings?
- Are your children eager to participate in these family activities and meetings?
- Are the meetings and activities exciting enough?
- What is the picture of your family that you would like to see in one year, five years, and ten years? What would it take to achieve those goals?

Initiate Involvement

Are you playing an active role in your family, or do you need to think of some new ways to start engaging family members in a more intentional manner? Invite individuals, or the whole family, to do something out of the ordinary: go to a museum or the fair, meet for coffee, offer to help with a garden project, attend a seminar together, or go to a play and talk about the substance of its plot afterwards. All these activities develop deeper relationships.

Reflect on Your Upbringing

Look at the families around you and at the same time consider your own response to how you were raised. It seems to me, most children grow up and become one of two things: a portrait of their own parents, or a reaction to them, causing them to swing dramatically to the other side and, for better or worse, change the way they will live and raise their own family. Really, we should do neither one. The best route is to develop a personalized plan for your family.

A happy family is but an earlier heaven.
~ George Bernard Shaw

Stages of Family Life – Part One

First comes love, then comes marriage,
then comes baby in a baby carriage.

When I was in high school my 1939 Ford was quite a car. Through a lot of elbow grease, I brought it to the standards of a high school boy in the 1950s. I had saved the money to purchase the car and did all the fixing up myself, so I was not going to waste a single day by not being behind the wheel of that classic beauty queen. My first drive would be to pick up Velda, my high school sweetheart.

Oh, how minutes can seem like hours to a teenage boy standing at the threshold of his sought-after freedom. The morning of my sixteenth birthday, Dad and I were first in line at the Washington State Drivers Licensing office when the doors opened. Big plans were ringing through my head for this day. Having a driver's license and the independence which came with it were near at hand. As soon as I passed the test and had the license in my wallet, I drove Dad downtown to the nearest bus stop so he could catch the next bus home and I could drive off on my own to accomplish my mission. My dad was such a great sport, he never made me feel like he was being put out or inconvenienced by taking the bus home that day.

I'll spare you the build up and just let you know, this was the day I "popped the question." Velda and I were too young for marriage, but we promised ourselves to each other for when the time was right. We had created a strong bond through our mutual activities in youth group, and a lot of time spent together with friends at my family's home. Even though we were very young, we both knew we wanted to build a life together. She said the magic word: "yes." We held the promise in our hearts and didn't announce our plans to anyone until after I graduated from high school, and even then, we waited on marriage until after my freshman year of college.

Velda and I had our first baby on July 2, 1956. Words do not describe the incredible feeling of being present in the delivery room when our baby girl came into this world. As each of our four children was born, it was love at first sight and an immediate bond occurred which took over every emotion I had. This was *our* child, *our* family, and the love was immeasurable. Every new parent and grandparent has that zinger of a moment when they look into that child's face for the first time and resolve to protect, love, and provide for that child forever.

Raising children teaches you a lot about yourself and offers an opportunity to enter into some of the most engaging relationships of a lifetime. It doesn't take being a parent for very long to realize that every single child is unique to the core. No two are created the same, so if you are parenting right now, you may be in completely uncharted territory! Take heart, it is the adventure of a lifetime. The more you invest in your family, the more valuable they become to you.

Reaping What We Sow

Like most new parents, Velda and I spent countless hours discussing our plans for each stage of our children's lives. As we understood it, our role was to draw out the quality and character that God had already planted within each of them. We knew that we had been blessed with great role models before us. While we wanted to include much of what we learned from them, we also had many of our own ideas that we wanted to incorporate.

The values we uphold to our children regularly include:

- Faith in God
- Forgiving attitudes
- The importance of education
- Living joyfully and embracing good humor
- Acceptance of all family members
- Commitment to marriage and healthy sexuality

Each stage of family life is unique and exciting when you take on an active, purposeful, and loving role. Author James Dobson wrote, "Children are not casual guests in our home. They have been loaned to us temporarily for the purpose of loving them and instilling a foundation of values on which their future lives will be built."

Looking back, I now see the generational links and realize that when you are raising and influencing your own children, you are also raising and influencing your grandchildren. If you want to see certain habits in your grandchildren, then you would be wise to start those habits developing in your own children. For example, if you want your grandchildren to treat you with respect, make certain you treat your own parents and grandparents with respect. This way your young children will pick up on this expectation and develop a good habit.

In the words of Billy Graham: "A child who is allowed to be disrespectful to his parents will not have true respect for anyone."

Modeling good habits will spread life lessons like wildflower seeds caught in the wind. You never know exactly when or where they will take root and bloom, but when they do, it is a beautiful thing.

Since we reap what we sow, Velda and I wanted to make sure we planted certain virtues to a depth that would take root and bloom again in the following generations. Families who pass along their deeply settled values will give strength and a firm foundation to following generations.

You Will Survive This!

Reality! The road you travel while parenting may take more out of you than you ever thought you had to give, but it will also fill you with the sweetest satisfaction you could ever imagine.

In one of her comedic monologues, actress Nicole Johnson quips, "Motherhood is hard. And I wish someone had told me that—not smiled and told me that, but sat me down, looked me square in the face, and said, 'You might not survive this.'"

But, we all do survive parenting and most will agree that we are better people for the experience. Your effort, guidance, and inspiration will give roots and wings to your children.

Whether your children are still in the sandbox or adults striking out on their own, parenting takes wholehearted devotion and should begin with a destination in mind. Influential parents work from a plan and keep to their priorities. Predetermine the experiences you want your family to have, choose carefully the mindsets you will attempt to develop in them, and be a person who follows through with your promises.

Promise Keeping Parents

We all know the feeling of being a young child and being told we were going to go and do something really special. Our minds would start creating the scenes as if we had already arrived, and the excitement would fill our bodies like helium in a balloon. Life would just have a lift to it as the countdown to the special event approached.

A close friend told me how his father would always make plans to do things and then not follow through. His father would remark glibly that their family would go fishing or to the lake on Saturday, but when the day rolled around he acted like he had never mentioned it. Because he grew up with a father who made a lot of plans and promises but never followed through, this young man was robbed of a meaningful relationship and confidence in the reliability of his father's words. Certainly, this father never realized the impact his broken promises had on his son over the years.

One time I told my friend I wanted to take him on a boat trip and laid out all the details for a great time together. As the time of the trip neared, I called his home to firm up some of the last minute details and was very surprised by his response. "Are we *actually* going to do this?" he asked. *Wham!* Impacting. I had no idea that the entire time we were talking about the trip, he thought we were just "talking" about it.

Children of all ages need to be able to count on their parents. They want to have confidence in our words and actions. If we say we are going to do something, we had better do it. Our follow-through serves as a great teacher of the importance of integrity. In contrast, empty promises, threats, and idle words are all teachers of distrust.

Unbreakable Gifts

For each of our granddaughters' 14th birthdays, my wife Esther handmade a one-of-a-kind doll, with a porcelain face and beautifully clothed in the likeness of that granddaughter. This was to be their "last doll" before growing up. Oh, the looks on the faces of these granddaughters as they opened the box in which their one-of-a-kind had been gently wrapped. I can just see each girl lifting her doll up into her arms and holding it with loving care, filled with love for her grandmother and for the lovely gift.

With incredible forethought, Esther pictured these porcelain dolls becoming a cherished heirloom and knew that they might, at some point in life, be accidentally broken. That being a reality, she wrote out a personal note to each of the girls and placed it inside the head of each doll. She did not tell the girls about this, but knowing if that day came, the granddaughter would be heartsick and feel guilty for allowing the gift to be broken. The note encouraged the granddaughter not to feel badly and explained that it was just a doll and things do break, but the gifts that don't break are the ones we have in our family and in our relationship with the Lord. Just for fun, Esther also wrote a few lines about what was going on in the life of that girl and a headline or two from current news events.

Just think of the deeper message in those notes. We want our children to know we value people more than we value things. While items will break, we work to ensure that our relationships will not.

Multiplying Factor

In a Family Circus cartoon, a probing, high-browed society woman looks upon a young mother with four children and asks, "How do you divide your love among four children?" The young mother answers, "I don't, I multiply it."

Have you ever heard a parent, usually one who is working long hours and spending extra time away from their children, say, "It isn't the quantity of time, it's the quality"? I say, it is both quantity and quality that counts. It takes time together to build memories, to pass on traditions and values, and to generally steer our children in the right direction. We love with our time

14

together, and, just like love, we need to look for ways to "multiply" our time.

My own father found ways of multiplying his time by often taking me along with him while he worked in the greenhouses, ran errands, or attended work parties at our church. This time afforded us the opportunity to build our relationship, as we had much time to talk during those rides in his truck and working side by side. I always felt like he enjoyed having me with him and I appreciate that he was creative in finding ways to connect with me.

Time and again the evenings would be spent at home with Dad down on the floor playing games with my brother and me until Mom realized the late hour and sent us all off to bed. My dad had so much gusto in him that he would work all day and still keep up with us kids, playing just as hard as we could.

My dad was never so locked into his personal time schedule that he would become ruffled by our interruptions or light-hearted shenanigans. One day when my older brother was home from college, he and I decided to pull a fast one on Dad. It was a cold day and Dad had to go out and check the thermostat in the greenhouses. While he was gone, my brother and I locked the front door to the house. When Dad came back, we heard the door rattle and awaited his response. Undeterred, Dad outsmarted us by climbing up the outside of the downspout to the second floor balcony. The window to the bedroom was unlocked, so my brother and I ran as fast as we could up the stairs to beat our dad to the unmanned entry. As we careened around the corner of the bedroom door, there was Dad, flying headlong through the bedroom window, landing on the bed with such a thud that it broke the wooden frame and the entire bed collapsed onto the floor!

The freedom to be spontaneous, silly, and generous with your time will keep you young at heart, and well connected to the pulse of the next generation.

Actions Express Priorities

The demands of balancing work and family are high. You need to work long and hard enough to keep up with the skyrocketing living expenses of a family but not to the detriment of your most precious asset, *your family*. The key is to maximize the hours you do have together and make sure you are using this time purposefully. This is accomplished by making family time a clear priority through limiting television viewing, turning off the electronic distractions, and engaging with your family in a way that tells them, *"You are important to me. I'm interested in you and I enjoy spending time with you."* Simply stated, unplug so you can reconnect with your family.

It could be our neurosis over work and responsibility that create the caving point in many families. The parent who throws his or her hands in the air in resignation declaring, "We can't afford to take time off work for a family vacation," may need to rethink that maybe they can't afford *not* to take time off for a family vacation. You see, the dilemma goes deeper than a shortage of time; it is a problem with priorities.

The late Stephen R. Covey said, "The key is not to prioritize what's on your schedule, but to schedule your priorities." This may be a hard first step for some, but it is crucial to your family's happiness and success. Decide what you want for your family, and decide what you will change in your current priorities.

Actions express priorities.
~ Mahatma Gandhi

Time Well Spent

- Be Present
  Attend all the plays, choir performances, sporting events, graduations, weddings, funerals, baptisms, confirmations, baby showers, and the like that you can. Demonstrate how happy you are to be there, and don't let your attitude show that you are rushed or would rather be someplace else. If you are there, be totally there, knowing that you are blessed to have family around you.

- Unplug
  Establish time when everyone turns off the electronics in the house and you just connect as a family. At the end of life, no one is going to wish they had watched more TV or played a few more online games.

- Put It on the Calendar
  Set dates for special events with individual family members and additional dates for the entire brood to get together.

Special Days

A man should never neglect his family for business.
~ Walt Disney

Years ago, I realized that if I don't make something part of my routine and put it on my calendar, I will never stick with it. If I was going to carry out some of the ideas I had for building my family, I would need to put those items on my business calendar and handle it with the same care, preparation, and importance as my other commitments – even more, really.

When my children were very young, I started giving each of them a "Special Day." I would block out half a day to spend with just one of my children. This was my chance to sit and listen to them and get to know what was going on inside their heads and hearts. It was always a great opportunity for that child to learn more about me, how I operate, what I care about, and above all, how much he or she means to me.

Together we ran errands, had a special lunch, went shopping, and talked about the things they were interested in. Often these days included an outward focus that involved delivering flowers to special teachers, mentors, or business clients. Special Days were put on the calendar and each child had their very own day twice a year. On their Special Day, I would wake that child by singing, *"Happy Wendy Day to you ..."* and tell them to dress nicely for our big day. If the child was school age, my wife would have called the teacher in advance to arrange for me to pick up the child midday from school. Even this part was strategic. I wanted them to go through the first part of the day experiencing the tickle in their stomach that a child feels when they are anticipating something special.

The most rewarding part about keeping this tradition over the years is now seeing our adult children celebrating "Special Days" with their own children and grandchildren. I hear stories of train rides, ski trips, days at the zoo, canoeing, bike rides, hikes, special luncheons, and more.

"Special Day" is a well-known term in our family, and reminiscing about those days is often the topic of conversation at family gatherings. Whether it is talk of visiting Santa when they were young, taking a train ride, or going to a fashion show, memories of the Special Days have become some of our family's favorite heirlooms.

Tips for Planning a Special Day
- The length of the day depends on the age of the child. For a young child, a few hours may be enough.

- The most important aspect is making the child feel special and loved.
- It's not about the event or the expense as much as it is about the one-on-one time. Quality age-appropriate conversation, and asking good questions to draw the child out regardless of age, will let them know you are interested in their world and their opinions.
- The bottom line is, what the mind of man can conceive, it can achieve. Put your creativity to work and make it a special time, filled with excitement and love!

It is important for children to be able to count on you for your word and the security that comes from being a part of traditions. When you create traditions like this, make sure you stick to them. If the need arises to change them, bring the child into the process of making the change. This way it feels like something new and positive rather than a disappointing letdown.

Tell Me a Story

I love to reminisce and imagine what life was like for those pioneers who forged through the wilderness in order to tame the land and settle out west. To this day, I can still imagine the sound of the strain on the wooden wheels of my great-grandparent's covered wagons as they crossed the barren prairies. I can hear the sloshing of the wagons through shallow river beds late at night to avoid unwanted advances of Indian tribes, and parents shushing the worn-out children longing for a rest from days of rough travel.

When I was a youngster, Great-Grandma Reynolds would often come to our house on Sunday afternoons. After dinner, she would fill my head with images of her childhood adventures.

Pulling me next to her, she would tell some of the most riveting and spine-tingling stories you can imagine. This was a total delight to the curious side of my boyish nature. I loved sitting with my great-grandma, and she never seemed to tire of all my questions about the olden days. I remember being on the edge of my seat with eyes wide and ears ablaze when she told me the story of the Indian raid she experienced while traveling across the country in a covered wagon. The Indians had never seen a blonde-haired child like her before. They all looked at her with great curiosity and moved in close to stroke her long golden strands. I could only imagine how frightening that must have been for her as a young girl.

Children have a strong appetite to hear the stories of the past. It is far more interesting to hear about the Flapper Generation from someone who lived it, and can remember the stylish way their parents would dress up, hit the town, and dance to the tunes of the big bands. From stories about displaced laborers living in tent cities called Hoovervilles, to WWII curfews and rations, sock hops, hippies and baby boomers, the younger generation will gain rich perspective from your stories and will grow to appreciate your generation.

Stories carry a uniqueness that allows us to touch all the generations. Stories honor the past generations by bringing meaning and perspective to their lives while appealing to the story-loving side of the younger generation. It is very important for parents and grandparents to indulge children with stories when they show interest. It is a way of drawing them in and presenting them with a treasure trove of adventure, humor, mystery, and family history.

Sitting with the children of our family on my lap, enthralled in family tales and asking for more, brings me great joy. To the youngest generation I will just be vaguely remembered, but with stories, I can engage them and our relationship has meaning.

Anchor Points

Story Telling Tips

- Tell short anecdotes and vignettes. If the kids ask more questions, keep talking, but in general keep the stories short and lively.
- Tell stories about the family when you were young. Children relate well to stories about people their own age.
- Show pictures and tell stories about the people and places.
- Follow the curiosity of the child. For example, a child asking a question like, "Grandpa, where did you get that old cash register?" can lead you to telling about how it was in your father's corner grocery store when you were their age.
- Demonstrate your enthusiasm for answering questions about family history and stories.
- Take the family on a tour of the neighborhood where you grew up and tell stories from your childhood.
- Not sure where to start with the stories? Play the Ungame®. This is a conversational game you can get on the internet, or make up your own playing cards. Each player picks a card that has a topic to talk about. Example: *Talk about the very first holiday you remember as a child.* The person holding that card simply tells their story. This game always launches questions, laughter, and more conversation.

Plan Coming of Age Celebrations

Plan age-appropriate activities to mark certain benchmarks in life. Parents and grandparents can both establish traditions for this, either separately or together. Here are ideas to help you get started forming your own.

- Five-year-olds can go on special trip with grandparents. Camping, Disneyland, Grand Canyon, or trekking the Lewis and Clark Trail. Do something memorable.
- For the ninth birthday, consider an overnight trip away with only Mom or only Dad.
- For kids 10 to 15 years of age, go to a fancy restaurant for the birthday celebration.
- The sixteenth birthday could be celebrated with all the women doing something memorable for the girl or the men doing a memorable activity for a boy.
  - Ladies: Go to a spa or create one at home; have a themed dinner party; include a scavenger hunt through the mall with dinner afterwards; have everyone write out what they appreciate most about this birthday girl and read them out loud.
  - Men: Go to a sporting event; have a backyard BBQ with yard games; go bowling or to a rodeo. Ask each of the men to share funny stories and good advice for the young man.
- Take an 18-year-old on a trip. Each family will have different budget parameters, but do your best to go all out. Save up and make it a memorable bonding time.

Daily Count Down!

For family still living in the same home:

- Five

  Five focused moments with the family you live with each day. Find a regular or predictable time or place where you can give a word of affirmation, ask caring questions, or give some encouragement:

  - in the car
  - at the doorway, coming or going from home
  - at the breakfast table

- Four

  Four hugs or points of touch per day.

- Three

  Three acts of kindness each week. Usually small and simple, but occasionally large and memorable. Find something to lighten another person's load or show that you thought of them.

- Two

  Two one-on-one meetings or "Special Days" per year.

- One

  One remark of gratitude per day. Do this at least once on the days you see family members who you don't live with.

Stages of Family Life – Part Two

As the Family Grows

Fathers will often stew about how they will handle the moment when some young man gets up the nerve to ask for his daughter's hand in marriage. Usually, the idea of letting him squirm is an enjoyable pastime for the father as the man in question nears the gut-wrenching moment when he must face the father and ask "the question." The question that rings some guys' bell like it was the knock-out round of a heavy weight championship. When it happened to me as a father, I saw the wind up; I was ready. The poor guy never saw what was coming.

The evening was moving on and we decided to recline in the living room after a satisfying dinner at home with our oldest daughter and her boyfriend, Bill. Sandy had been seeing Bill for quite some time, and it was clear the two of them were making long-term plans. Once we relocated to the living room, my daughter disappeared like a vapor behind her mother to help clean the kitchen. Immediate suspicion settled over me. This was the moment. This was the set-up. I gave the young prospect an unassuming glance and left the ball in his court. He began to fidget as he built up the courage, and finally the question came.

"What would you think of Sandy and me getting married? I mean, I would like to ask for her hand in marriage."

25

"Hmmm ..." I mulled over the request with practiced contemplation and shot back a question of my own. "What do you think of premarital sex?" I had knocked him off balance with a hook shot he was not expecting, but this gave way to a very open conversation.

After a few seconds of intense pressure, we both had a good laugh and felt the openness to enter into a more relaxed conversation about building toward their future together. This was the whole point, taking down walls so I could have open communication with my future son-in-law.

A few years later, the next prospective son-in-law came to me and I asked him the same question. He smiled knowingly and said, "Bill told me you would have a few good questions for me."

These young men were about to become important members of my family, and I wanted to break the ice early on. It was not my place to poke around in their marriages, but it was my job to prepare them and encourage them, to the best of my ability.

It was very important to my first wife, Velda, that whenever someone married one of our children, we would not consider that person to be set apart as an "in-law." Rather we would view them as another one of our children. In a similar desire for family unity, my second wife Esther and I agreed that we would not use the term "step" when referring to family members. Instead we would refer to both sides of our blended family as "our children" and "our grandchildren." No divisions, just acceptance and a purposeful communication of our desire to have a close relationship with each and every family member.

Anticipate the Finer Things to Come

Marriage and family are places where many people incur deep wounds and hefty disappointments. We have all heard stories of disapproval, hurtful words, rejection, and unnecessary breaking of relationships that lead to despair for married couples and confusion in children. Families will change, and our roles change as we age. We have a choice: We can embrace these changes as blessings or we can oppose them with caustic bitterness. Everyone wins when we receive these inevitable changes with anticipation for the finer things to come.

Changing Roles

Looking across the table at my friend Jim, as his tired eyes sank to his coffee cup, I could tell the night before had been long and rough. He told me of sitting up late into the night in the hospital with his aging mother, back-to-back with getting his daughter off early in the morning to cheerleading camp. I could relate, as I was entering the same season of life: a season now called the "sandwich generation."

This is when you find yourself in mid-life dealing with the many needs of your own aging parents while you still have children of your own at home. The sandwich generation spends their time parenting both up and down the generations and can feel overwhelmed as they attempt to do their best for both ends of the family. This is a time when things are coming at you so fast you feel like you are in a revolving door that is spinning around too rapidly to get out.

Eventually, the time will come when you change roles with your children, and if you live long enough, your grandchildren. When this time comes, it is important to recognize the strength and wisdom in allowing this to happen, and to grant permission for those roles to change by asking advice or handing over responsibility to a younger family member.

When my first wife died, I realized my emotions were such that I was not able to continue running my company and making business decisions while I was grieving. I called upon my son and asked him to take over daily operation of the business and gave him authority to do so. I'm sure handing that role off to Steve was a confidence builder for him. It conveyed the message that I saw him as completely ready for such a task.

As a word of caution, we should look upon those who are younger than us for their actual capabilities and not get hung up, as some are in the habit of doing, with the personal deficiencies only a family member can see. People tend to rise to the level of confidence we place in them.

I remember well these role-changing times with my own parents. On one occasion, I took my mother to the doctor for a checkup where I heard her telling the doctor that she was having no trouble at all. I interjected, "Mom, what about those dizzy spells from last week?" "Oh, yes! I forgot about that," she said.

The adult child may realize when the time for assistance has come before the aging parent is willing to relinquish control. It is always best for the parent to offer this role-change early on, but when it is not offered, the adult child should gently tell the parent that it is time and do everything possible to ensure their dignity. Whether it is suggesting the time has come to stop driving, move to an assisted living facility, or to accept help with managing doctor appointments, you are protecting your parent when you step into this new role.

In the event that your role-changing and family-growing experience is far more complicated and riddled with stress, it may be a good idea to seek out guidance from a good counselor. You could even try this online blog, www.girlfriendswithagingparents.com, where many in the Sandwich Generation are pooling their ideas and encouragement for dealing well with family situations and dynamics. It says "girlfriends," but I'm sure they wouldn't turn away a guy with questions or insight either.

Assisting Aging Family Members

As our parents' memory capacity and hearing both fade with age, the need will arise for a spouse or adult child to accompany them to the doctor. There are important details discussed at these appointments which will be better understood and followed up on when another person is also responsible for listening. If you have a large family, it is best to assign one or two people to the job of accompanying Mom or Dad to the doctor. Too many different people helping with this task can cause its own confusion.

In addition, no family member should be left alone in a hospital or medical facility. It is always best to have someone who has knowledge of the patient's medical history (medicines, intolerances, blood type, etc.) checking over things.

Helping with Financial Management

Eventually the day comes when responsible adult children need to have access to the checking accounts, and they should be made aware of all financial assets and passwords. Insurance paperwork, wills, estate planning, and keeping track of bills are other areas where the aging family member will need the assistance of a kindhearted younger person. Financial details can be overwhelming and aging parents can lapse into financial distress if another set of eyes is not watching over the details.

Loss of a Loved One

Sooner or later everyone will know the common human experience of grief. My first-hand experience came without warning on a Thanksgiving evening. My wife Velda and I had enjoyed a family dinner at the home of our daughter Sandy and her husband Bill. We were ready to leave early in the morning for a fun-filled trip with our daughter Wendy and her husband Mike. Our bags were packed and set by the door in anticipation of leaving the next morning for southern California where we would shake off the early winter cold with a sunny vacation. The four of us finished off the evening with a late night movie and headed to bed. We wanted to be well-rested for our big plans the next day. Those plans were changed by the most traumatic event of my life.

After falling asleep for a short while, I awoke to hear my wife's labored breathing and instantly knew we were in serious trouble. I yelled to the kids to call 911 and immediately began CPR with the support of my son-in-law Mike. The EMTs did all they could, including rushing her to the hospital, but my wife of thirty-one years was pronounced dead without warning or good-byes.

I returned from the hospital shocked and stunned by the loss of my soul mate. At the age of fifty, I found myself feeling lonely and insecure without her words of affirmation, her advice, and the balance that can only come from a committed relationship with someone you love and respect. Many friends and members of our extended family rallied to support the children and me.

The rest of the holidays, which Velda had always made so special, and the months that followed were very difficult as our family worked through our grief. Our family's strong foundation, faith in God, and philosophy of sticking together and supporting each other through the good, the bad, and the ugly, held us together through this time.

Some of the best advice I received came from my psychiatrist friend, Dr. Alan Cook, who visited me the day after Velda's death. He explained that this was the worst tragedy I would probably ever experience. He also suggested I recognize that, for a time, I would actually be impaired, but assured me that time is a great healer. He explained that the waves of emotion would roll over me and mow me down like great ocean waves, but as time went on, the waves would be spaced further apart and become less intense.

Realizing the truth in his words, I turned all the business operations over to my family and staff while I took steps to grieve my loss and get my bearings, wondering what my new life would be like. The effect of the shock numbed my senses; I functioned as though I was in a fog, just going through the motions of daily living. After the dullness subsided and feelings returned, the most important factor was to work through the steps of grief which cannot be ignored. Do not try to ignore grief; I found it was vital to a healthy recovery.

The grief process, says Elisabeth Kubler-Ross, is a five-stage process: denial, anger, bargaining, depression, and finally acceptance. That's how we grieve; it is also how we accept, forgive, and respond to the many changes life throws our way.

Although the five-step process looks tidy on paper, it is not tidy in life. We do not move through it in a compartmentalized manner. I floundered through, fighting the feelings, with much backward movement until I reached that peaceful state called acceptance.

Anchor Points

Welcome New Family Members

Create a unique tradition for letting new family members know they are a valued part of your core family. It could be a special gift which is given to each new spouse of your children. It could be an initiation day, where a group of you go out and welcome in the new member with a fun activity, laughter and good times. Whatever you choose, the point is to sincerely roll out the welcome mat.

Encourage Talk Time

Fill a bowl with slips of paper with different questions on them. While sitting around the table after dinner or gathered in the living room, ask everyone to draw a question and answer it. Here are some sample questions, but more can be found online.

- If you could be successful at anything, what would it be?
- What was your favorite holiday as a child and why?
- Who is someone you have always wanted to meet?
- What were your grandparents like?
- What is something you have done that makes you feel good about yourself?
- Describe your ideal birthday.
- What do you like to do when you are alone?
- What angers you the most?
- Who was really special to you as a child and why?
- If this were your last year to live, how would you want to spend it?

- If you could successfully change one thing that is wrong in this world, what would that be?
- What do you like to daydream about?
- Tell about a time you were lost. What did you do and how did you feel?
- What is the best advice you have ever received?
- What do you see yourself doing in five years?

Do Family Research

See if anyone would be interested in joining you to do some genealogy research. Starting out with a juicy bit of family history could pique their interest, so you may need to do a bit of research first to encourage other family members to get involved.

Create a Family Crest

Provide all the necessary supplies to decorate a family crest. It could be at the simple craft level or something you all work on and have cast in metal. Create a crest with symbols and words that have meaning for your family. This could be an evening project at home or an activity at a family gathering where each family within the big family makes their crest and shares its meaning with the larger group.

Assist Aging Parents

When their health begins to decline, and hopefully before their memory does the same, start accumulating information that will be instrumental in helping you take care of them in the best possible way. Include bank accounts, passwords, investments, doctor's names, and lists of medications. If they have not yet done so, help them to write a will and appoint a power of attorney for a time when they won't be able to make decisions.

Connect with a grandparent by:
- Driving them places, if they are no longer able to drive.
- Doing some of their yard work.
- Deep cleaning their house or doing a project they don't have the strength or focus to handle.
- Going to the store and running errands for them.
- Taking them to visit a friend or family.
- Offering assistance with the computer and new technologies.

Grandparents love to be asked to help out. Ask them to:
- Bake cookies for an event.
- Use their home for entertaining.
- Take a grandchild to a class.
- Share a family recipe with you.
- Share their opinion on something important.
- Attend special celebrations.
- Tell you what it was like when they were young, newly married, buying a house, facing a hardship, etc.

Plan Multi-Generational Outings
Keep in mind ages, interests, and physical needs of everyone attending. Babies need a quiet place for naptime, the teens and young adults want excitement like rock climbing or water skiing, while the grandparents just want to be close to see everyone. Shoot for outings that consider everyone's needs.

Example: A lakefront with large shade trees for a family picnic where the older ones can sit in lawn chairs, play croquet with the youngsters and take gentle walks, while watching the young adventure seekers paddle their kayaks, jump off the high dive, or water ski. Everyone can have fun and be comfortable together. This is the ideal type of family event setting.

Answer Telephone Calls Cheerfully

Always sound happy to hear a family member's voice on the other end of the phone. Pay attention to the sound of your voice. Tone sends more of a message than do your actual words.

Accentuate the Positive

We Put Each Other Up

Home. What images come to mind when you think of that word? I don't know why I set myself up like this, but when the kids were young, I somehow always had this Norman Rockwell image of what home life would look like inside my front door when I arrived from a long day at the office. One day I opened the front door to discover my twelve-year-old daughter, Kathy, raking my son, Steve, over the coals. Volume elevated, fire in her eyes, my sweet little girl was taking her brother to task and reminding him of his lowly position in the world. Quickly glancing around the room, I did recognize the furniture and a few wall hangings, so I had some confirmation that I had entered the correct house. Reminding myself that we always praise in public and reprimand in private, I said, "Kathy, come with me." We walked into her bedroom where I began my fatherly investigation of the hullabaloo I had just witnessed.

> *Don't have anything to do with foolish and stupid arguments; because you know they produce quarrels.*
> ~ 2 Timothy 2:23

I sat down on her bed so I would be at eye level with her and asked, "Kathy, what was going on out there? I thought in our family we look for ways to put each other up."

With vehemence in her voice, my dear little daughter declared, "*NOT HIM!* You are always putting him up. Somebody's got to *bring him down* once in a while."

Our best laid plans don't always produce the qualities we intend. Press on, it will come.

There is enough influence in our society seeking to tear a person down. In our family, we emphasize the importance of building each other up with positive and loving words of affirmation and encouraging physical touch. Sometimes just putting your arm around someone's shoulder or squeezing a hand will say far more than words ever could.

Habits Slip off the Tongue

Careless, hasty statements will break the backbone of any family. Many families have caused pain because they have developed, even honed, a habit of putting each other down. It becomes their normal, everyday interaction, and they don't even realize this habit has gone too far. Think of this as toxic talk which is poison to the soul. Everyone needs to have a safe haven, a place where they know they have people who will speak well of them and lift them up with encouraging words and an assuring pat on the back. That place should be home: a place of refuge, acceptance, humor, and love. This is the essence of family.

Just like water wearing away at a rock, constantly dripping positive affirmations into each person's life will erode negative influences while creating a crevasse for positive self esteem to sink in. Our words to our family should continually whisper, *"You can do it – you've got this – if it doesn't work out we are here for you – we love you.*" This should be the habit that slips off our tongues.

At the end of the day, our verbal cues should spur our children on to deep feelings of assurance and bolster their confidence to pursue their dreams. A family that builds a strong community within itself, where people are built up with joy and celebration, will be a family with a tight bond and many magical moments.

Family Self-Talk

I don't remember many of the presents I received as a child, but I do remember the many gifts of positive words my parents gave so generously.

"You are the luckiest kids around to have a mother as sweet and beautiful as yours." Dad reminded us often of how blessed we were. Affirming words about our family were so easy for Dad to speak. He didn't have to think hard to muster something good to say, he just made a habit of speaking well, and we picked up on his example. He painted the word picture, and it became our reality. Matching his attitude, Mom always let us know how much she respected Dad and bragged about his work projects.

Listen and hear what other people are saying about their families. Some of it will be distressing, but hopefully others will speak well and hold high opinions. Either way, let your listening build an awareness of the striking potency of our spoken words.

We have all heard the careless murmurs accompanied by looks of disapproval. "*My family is so dysfunctional.*" "*My family never does anything fun.*" "*I can't count on my family for anything.*" And on it goes. These words become our beliefs after a while, and what we believe becomes our reality. Reckless words pierce like a sword and undermine the potential within a family.

Strong families make a habit of speaking well about how their family operates. Words trigger pictures and those pictures tie to emotions within us regarding our family relationships and experiences. How about making it your purpose to praise your family as a whole and not hold back words of confidence in them.

Our family mantra is: "In our family we look for ways to put each other up."

Make invigorating statements like, "*Our family has a great sense of humor*" or "*Our family always sticks together.*" As the adults make deposits of positive and affirming statements into the family a routine, the younger ones pick up the habit.

As these words take on life, they will intertwine the generations and send profound blessings both up and down the generations. A child who easily says, "Our family is very supportive," may find that this openness to family support returns to him as a blessing in a practical way. It could be that when something happens, like an accident or loss of a job, the parents and grandparents are there to offer words of understanding and possibly even a little financial support to hold things together in the short term. At another time, these same grandparents may experience similar support returning to them when a couple broad-shouldered grandsons show up to chop and stack wood on the weekend. They may even say something like, "Grandma and Grandpa do so much for us, we are happy to give them a hand."

Just make this the common habit your family rolls with. Positive talk is a cross-directional, multiplying, and renewable resource.

The Meaning in Our Words

I'm going to make a new rule: Grandparents are allowed to eavesdrop. Not because we want to know all the scuttlebutt; I just find myself enjoying listening to the stories chattering between family members on all sorts of different occasions. Graduations, weddings, family gatherings for any reason or no reason at all; they are all nice opportunities to listen in on family conversations because these conversations allow me to listen into their hearts.

My son Steve and his beautiful wife Jewell did a splendid job of raising three high-spirited and delightful daughters. When the girls were little, the movie *Toy Story* was a big deal and playacting some of their favorite characters like Buzz Lightyear, who was ready and capable of bringing order to save the universe, was a great pastime. Their family made a game of snuggling and playing with the girls in the evenings; this would often lead to attempts to outdo one another with love. One would say something like, "I love you more than ice-cream." Trying to top that one, another would say, "I love you more than a million dollars," and on it would go, until the one who would not be outdone would shout, "I love you *to infinity and beyond!"*

This word picture became such a part of their family's affirming talk that Steve and Jewell had each of the girls design her own ring with the center of it being the infinity symbol. The rings were given to the girls at a special time in their lives to represent the love and support that would always be lavished on them by their family, and also as a commitment ring to uphold a promise to remain pure until their own wedding day.

Their oldest daughter Chelsea and her husband Adam were married in a picturesque historic mansion in their home town. The congratulatory tone somehow mingled with the fresh air and wafted gently through the host of high-spirited guests. One would think the day could not have been topped after seeing the stunning bride and groom join their lives in a truly memorable ceremony; little did we all know there was a crescendo yet to come.

In a bustling courtyard, among joyful guests and glasses ready to be lifted high in a toast to their future together, my son, the father of the bride, brought all attention to this lovely couple with a show-stopping toast. Steve expressed his abounding joy in raising Chelsea and his great confidence in Adam and hope for their future together, but the moment that took our breath away was wrapped in the last sentence when Steve lifted his glass to toast his daughter and son-in-law and said these words, "I will always love you, to infinity and beyond."

In that moment, my heart swelled almost beyond composure with the pride I felt for the loving father my son is to his own family. I have always loved and admired my son, but in that moment, it was *to infinity and beyond!*

Write it Down

Don't you love that feeling of finding a personal little handwritten note, scrawled out just for you? A lot of moms and dads are good about putting little notes like this in lunch bags or backpacks with words to encourage their child throughout the day. *Good luck on your spelling test! I know you will do well.* Or a simple, *I love you, I'm proud of you, looking forward to afterschool cookies with you today.* People often speak nice words, but it takes effort to put them in writing—and putting them in writing makes a stronger commitment to those words.

No matter the age, everyone feels a lift when finding a note placed somewhere for their surprise. A husband who runs his hand into his pants pocket and finds a piece of paper with a note saying, "*Thanks for being such a good man,*" will feel loved and appreciated, and a wife who finds a note stuck to her favorite coffee cup will feel valued.

At one time, I had to be out of town for an extended stay, but wanted my wife to feel uplifted and appreciated during my absence. I sat down and wrote out several short messages on post-it-notes and enlisted the help of our daughter, Phyllis, to sneak into the house and place them in strategic locations for Esther to find. Knowing she would have to wind the grandfather clock, I had Phyllis place a note on one of the chimes that read, "Whatever time it is, Phil loves Esther." Another note went on the rear view mirror in her car with the words, "I adore the woman you are looking at." These are the smaller incidental, yet still very important, written words.

On a much larger scale, our daughter Cheryl and her husband Neil have a graduation tradition that absolutely thrills me. They have a manner of impressing the graduate with strong affirming words and reminders of how rich life has been during their school years.

After all, high school graduation is a twelve-year collection of late nights spent helping with class projects, anxiety over finals, and countless miles in the seat of the family taxi. It's memories of all the times you stood up for this kid, cheered for his team, wiped her tears, and held both the disappointments and victories as if they were your very own.

When the heart can't contain the joy of those memories, it is a good idea to put all those culminating thoughts on paper where it can be read for years to come. This will serve as a later reminder of how special he or she is to you and how you, as the parents, have cherished the memories.

Standing in their family room with a large crew gathered around, Cheryl and Neil pulled out the well-drafted letter and prepared to read it to the graduate. The emotion and memories surged through all of our minds.

Theirs is a family that lives a fully engaged life, creating special memories and valuing the uniqueness of each member. Mom and Dad took turns reading the letter they composed just for the graduate, reminiscing about the poignant moments and events that gave definition to their relationship. Sprinkled with a bit of good-natured ribbing and reminders of benchmarks in life, these letters will be a cherished possession for each of these children.

The following is a portion of one of these letters:

Words from Mom:

...So, Cameron, as you enjoy this last summer before you set off on your next big feat – Gonzaga – Engineering – Honors – or whatever venture you decide to embark on – know that you have been our treat. We are so proud of you and all you have accomplished so far and look forward to where life will take you.

Words from Dad:

... I love watching you figure things out [at work], sometimes it's the proper way to do something. Sometimes it's about collaborating with those around you. The challenges will keep coming, you'll keep things handled.

As with your sister and brother who have gone before you, I am so excited about all the things you've done to get to this point, being your father has been a privilege and an honor. Your future is bright; I can hardly wait to watch! I am your biggest fan!

Listening as the graduation letter is read reminds me of what's valuable in life: taking time for purposeful and multiple connections with family members where we put down firm roots, stabilize broad wings, and offer resonating words of affirmation.

Whether it is a note slipped under someone's pillow, a few lines of affirming words in a birthday card, an encouraging speech given at a special occasion, or a message printed atop the family calendar, meaningful words put into writing will carry a lot of power as they infuse the relationship with sincerity.

"Oh, Boy!"

You provide children with a good home, a nice bedroom, warm meals and fireside chats; what do they really want? The pirate's life! Filled with swashbuckling fun, and no one keeping tabs on bed time!

As a family endeavor, we operated Camp Harmony on Stuart Island in the San Juans. Adventure and inspiration were lavished on hundreds of guests who came for a transforming camp experience.

Our family's favorite camp experience featured a swashbuckling pirate theme, where three generations of family walked the gangway to become marooned pirates for a weekend, complete with costumes, treasure hunts, and a pirate ship parade on the high seas. Okay, it was a bunch of private decorated dinghies tied end to end in a small cove, but to us, it was the high sea!

One of our granddaughters, who is now an adult, told us how she loves to be near the ocean and to smell the salt water, because it always takes her back to the excitement of standing on the dock, waiting for the boat to arrive and take her away to another Camp Harmony experience.

Staffing for Camp Harmony was straight forward. We looked for counselors with an "oh, boy!" attitude. If a camp counselor was leading a group of kids through the woods and it started to rain, we didn't want a leader who would get irritated with the circumstances or give up and head back to camp. We wanted someone who would say, "Oh, boy! Now we get to build a lean-to for shelter. Let's find some branches!"

When individuals see opportunities instead of road blocks, they bring a dynamic spirit of enthusiasm which spreads to the people around them. Rubbing shoulders with "oh, boy!" attitudes opens the eyes of the individual to see creative opportunities and encourages possibility-thinking as a way of life. These people are out there. Find them. Then, get them acquainted with your family.

When we find someone with an "oh, boy!" attitude, we will have them over for dinner, invite them on a family weekend, or meet for lunch. Doing life with people who breathe contagious enthusiasm is an effective way of infusing your family with the same gusto for life.

The Key

Too often people get comfortable with their attitude and lug around a negative view of their own family. When these negative thoughts are given a voice, they become a lid which keeps the family down and suppresses the potential for change and growing relationships.

This is the key: If you want your family to connect and be interested in you and in each other, get excited about them and about whatever it is they find exciting.

Show your interest in being a part of their lives and invite them on adventures to create lasting memories and growth opportunities. They will join your enthusiasm when you engage in their interests and cheer them on to victory in the things they find important. In practical terms, show up, cheer them on, and whenever possible, provide assistance when requested.

"Burple"

Engaging the silly bone in a family is like pouring syrup over pancakes: it is simply the best part. Family gatherings, where the spontaneous combustion of laughter roars through the living room, are my idea of a slice of heaven. If it will bring joy or create smiles, laughter, and good memories, our family is all in.

I guess I come by this naturally because both my parents sported a quick-witted funny bone. The church I grew up in had a practice of making a decision only after every member had a chance to vote on it. Even changing the color of the carpet in the sanctuary had to go before a congregation-wide vote.

The large double doors to the church building were propped open and several members had already arrived. This was the night of the all-important vote on the color of new carpet, and if you wanted your voice known, you would be there early to place your tally mark on the large board next to the color of your preference: gray, green, or beige. Most had already used the oversized black marker to place their vote and were now mingling around the sanctuary, getting ready for the evening service. After the service we would hear the announcement on the winning color.

Oddly, it turned out the winning color, by a landslide, was "burple." Burple had far more votes than any other, which created some tension and chatter among those who had never heard of such a color and felt strongly about using a more neutral shade. Evading anyone's notice, my dad had snuck over, written in the new color, and tally marked it with enough votes to win! We laughed all the way home and to this day it is one of our favorite stories to share with family.

The "Philbert Award"

Keeping up with the tradition of family merriment, each summer my wife and I invite our adult grandchildren and their spouses to a special location for "Grandkid Weekend." The weekend is filled with equal portions of nonsense and sincerity. It tickles me to see these grandkids when they come together. There is always a rush of energy wrapped in hugs and lively chatter. Oh, there are some who are a bit more reserved who show their enthusiasm in a more low-key manner. We wouldn't be a family without a blend of personalities, and we want everyone to feel like they can be themselves.

Everyone seems to have a ball on these annual weekends because fun and humor are at the core of the master plan. To keep us humble, and as a means of catching up on each other's lives, we have introduced the highly sought after "Philbert Award." This is a traveling trophy (a sales award I won over fifty years ago) that is awarded to the person who tells the most outrageous story about the "dumbest" thing he or she did during the previous year. Laughter, gasps of horror, and "attaboy" slaps on the back fill the air as each one tries to outdo the other. The grandkids are the ones who named the award, and each year the winner really deserves the high honor.

True stories of precarious situations with lock-outs, rolled cars, and great ideas gone awry are not in short supply from these grandkids. One granddaughter used her sign language skills to communicate with a customer at her store who, it turned out, was not actually deaf! Another granddaughter locked herself out of her house one morning, and had to muster up the courage to go meet her new neighbors clad in her pajamas and slippers. The zinger this year had to be from our grandson Daniel, who saw a tired looking man leaning against a building and assumed he was homeless. Daniel took a twenty-dollar bill out of his wallet and handed it to the man saying, "Thank you for not asking for money. I hope this helps." As he walked off with his wife, she looked at Daniel and said, "Honey, he wasn't homeless." Turns out he was just a tired employee taking his break on the back steps of the building, but I'm sure he enjoyed telling the story to his family when he got home!

The looks on the faces of their cousins, the "voting audience," are often of complete astonishment. Usually, an explosion of laughter will blast through the living room as our winner is declared! With dignity and poise the winner comes forward to receive the not-so-coveted award. It really is an honor just being nominated for the Philbert!

Serious Fun

Laughter spawns all sorts of great chemical reactions within the body, and sharing laughter with others is one of life's greatest pleasures. I feel for parents and grandparents who are too reserved to push out the boundaries, take risks, and do really fun things together with all the generations invited. Silly capers are some of the most engaging experiences where walls are taken down, pride is set aside, and close connections are made.

When my dad took my brother and me out to work in the greenhouses during the summer, we would often wear a "side arm" filled with water to soak the other when he was unaware. Then a bucket of water hurled on an unsuspecting victim would begin a water war with our only defense being fast feet or a garbage can lid as a shield. Even work could be seriously fun.

Life has enough competition and stress built in. Purposefully adding some high-spirited hoopla to any ordinary day is a healing and energizing agent for your family. When we take our family "Goofy Bowling," it is an intentional set-up to handicap their skills and create laughter. We don't need an atmosphere of serious competition; we need an atmosphere of serious fun.

Meaningful Touch

Always kiss your children goodnight, even if they're already asleep.
~ H. Jackson Brown, Jr.

When my father passed away, I quickly became aware that
my seventy-two-year-old mother was not only suffering the loss
of the man who was the love of her life, but she was also no
longer receiving the constant physical touch that he had lavished
on her their entire married life. This hit me as too much of an
emotional loss for Mom, and I decided to make a point of giving
her lots of physical affection when we were together.

The warmth of another person's touch brings security and
love in a way that words are inadequate to convey. Everyone
needs to be touched. Researchers have found profound health
and relationship benefits from the simple act of hugging. Hugging
breathes fresh life into our tired bodies and shows another person
how much we care about their well-being. A big bear hug will
break down walls and send a message of acceptance straight to
the heart, boosting self esteem and bringing about a sense of full
acceptance.

Moms tend to be natural-born huggers. And while more dads
often struggle with hugging, it is not something to avoid. It is
crucial to the relational and personal development of each child
to be embraced daily by each of their parents. Say "good
morning" with a hug and say "good night" with a hug. Say
"thank you" with a hug and offer encouragement and
congratulations with a hug.

Many scientific researchers report similar findings on
hugging:

- More upbeat moods
- Reduced heart rates
- Lower blood pressure

- Increased nerve activity
- Reduced levels of cortisol (Cortisol is a stress hormone. When cortisol dips, there's a surge of two "feel good" brain chemicals, serotonin and dopamine.)

Don't Touch Me!

Have you ever come in contact with a young teenager who has adamantly decided that he or she doesn't like to be touched or hugged, especially in public? Certainly most adolescents go through a time when they are uncomfortable in their own skin, but saying they don't want to be touched isn't really conveying the heart of the matter.

Actually, we all need to be touched in appropriate and meaningful ways every day. Dr. Bhagat, a noted psychiatrist based in Delhi, India, makes this statement about physical touch: "Touch is an important component of attachment as it creates bonds between two individuals." I definitely want to create those bonds with my family and for them to see me as a warm, affectionate parent and grandparent. Hugging is simply a natural expression of showing that you love and care.

If anything, young people in this stage need even more acceptance and an outward display of love and affection. I've heard many people say we should respect their wishes and not touch them at all. I differ on this and suggest taking an alternate route. When the normal hugs are pushed away, try a different route, but don't walk away.

We need four hugs a day for survival.
~ Virginia Satir, family therapist

My father used to wrestle with my brother and me on the living room floor in the evenings while playing marbles, and he included a lot of pats on the back for a good shot. A friend of mine used to chase her two boys around the house yelling, "Mommy's germs, no returns!" The boys clearly loved being chased around furniture and over countertops, but always seemed to "trip" over something to allow the assailant to apprehend them and engulf them in a full tackle.

Touch and affirmation are vital parts of delivering the blessing that says, "You are special and I'm committed to you."

With all the media reports of child abuse, inappropriate touching, and sexual harassment, we've backed away from touch even more in our society. We need to realize, however, that avoiding healthy, appropriate, meaningful touch sacrifices physical and emotional health in our lives and the lives of our loved ones.

Try some of these alternative approaches to affirming with appropriate and acceptable touch:

- Scratch his or her back
- High five
- Knuckle bump
- Thumb fight
- Comb or braid hair
- Arm wrestle
- Pat a hand when dropping off a lunch or book
- Play tag or other games that include a bit of physical touch
- Offer to rub a sore muscle
- Set up a three-legged race
- Have a poke war. See who can be the last one to poke each other. Kids do this all the time with their friends.

Even if some of these alternatives are rejected, remember that it is a privilege to help young people through this stage in life. They may not mention it out loud, but they will notice your consistency and care.

Free-flowing Blessings

Whether it is through your spoken words or appropriate physical touch, you have the ability to give something that every child longs for and every friend, spouse, and neighbor would appreciate deeply. This is something that has been practiced through Jewish culture back to ancient times, and it is still as fresh and necessary today. It is given through words of affirmation and appropriate physical touch; it opens up relationships and uplifts those who receive it. It is a sturdy foundation of love and acceptance, and it is clear when it is being given. It is a blessing.

For those we love most, our blessing conveys a message of acceptance and belonging which is irreplaceable in this world awash with uncertainty and rejection.

Because the hunger for affirmation and acceptance runs deeply in human nature, it will be sought after and found, even if it comes from ill-gotten means. Gangs, cults, and the neighborhood bar all offer their own brand of "family" and acceptance. That type of dark refuge is a sad counterfeit for the genuine love that comes from a parent or grandparent's meaningful touch and words that press love, acceptance, and high value into their hearts.

Spoken Blessings

Our words should be as apples of gold in settings of silver.
~ Proverbs 25:11

When we speak highly of our children by saying things like, "You are so good about putting other people first," we find that they fulfill those words. Their brains ping with positive, pleasurable feedback that makes them want to live up to such a reputation, and they strive to become truly kind people. The child who grows up hearing, "You are just a bad seed and lazy," will usually live up to that expectation as well. Our words are powerful and capable of changing the course of history when we take the time to speak life-giving, affirming words into the lives of our loved ones.

Let's not vandalize the precious gift of family with sour, hurtful words which tear down the structure of our lives. Words aptly spoken stir up vitality, which is life giving, healing, and relationship building.

Personally, I deeply appreciate it when my children and grandchildren send a card, make a phone call, email, text or just turn to me with thoughtful words. Words that bless, like a powerful magnet, pull people in and make a firm attachment.

Anchor Points

Ponder These Questions

The extent to which you can answer these questions will reveal where your values really are.

- What is your family worth to you?
- What is your current opinion of your family?
- How would you like to see that opinion changed?
- What is your plan to affect change in your family? Be specific and realistic in your answer.
- How would you like to see your family in five years? What needs to be accomplished to get your family to that goal?

Practice Positive Talk

Practice positive verbal and internal talk.

- Self Talk
  - "I value my family."
  - "I enjoy spending time with my family."
  - "I love doing things for and with my family."
  - "I look for teachable moments."
  - "I make time for my family."
  - "I look for creative activities for my family."
- Family Talk
  - "Our family looks for ways to put each other up."
  - "Our family is very supportive of each other."
  - "Our family always helps each other out."
  - "Our family is very close."
  - "Our family cares about the community."
  - "Our family has a great sense of humor."
  - "Our family is fun."

Strive for Multiple Communications

Find several different ways of sending uplifting messages to your family.

- Face-to-face, one-on-one, or in a crowd, create multiple opportunities to engage with your family and to lift each other up.
- Remember birthdays, anniversaries, promotions, etc., and call or get together to celebrate those occasions.
- Notice when someone is struggling and offer help.
- Propose a toast to a person for a special accomplishment when a few others are around to hear the good words and join in the good vibes.
- Use affirmations.
    - "I really enjoy spending time with you."
    - "I noticed how thoughtful you were in that situation."
    - "I sure appreciate your help with this project."
    - "I love it when you _____."
    - "I noticed something I can learn from you."
- Leave notes with encouraging words. Post-it notes work great for this.
    - On the bathroom mirror: "I sure love the person you are looking at."
    - Inside a math book: "Proud of all your studying for this test. We'll have your favorite dinner tonight."
    - On a rearview mirror: "Can't wait to see you tonight!"
    - Inside a jacket pocket: "Thank you for mowing the lawn. You are so dependable."
    - Inside a baseball mitt: "Go get 'em slugger. Ice cream after the game!"

- Send a note or letter the old fashioned way, through the mail. It will be a welcome gift nestled among all the bills and junk mail.
- Email, text, and use social networking.
  Not everyone in the older generation is quite comfortable with technology yet, but if your grandchildren are using it, this is your ace-in-the-hole for speaking their language today.
    o Send an emoticon
    o XOXO
    o I'm proud of you!
    o I love you.
    o Got time for coffee?
    o Thinking of you today.

Put it on Display
Proudly place all awards, certificates, or special projects where they can be seen by all. The family wall of fame is usually the refrigerator, fireplace mantel, or bulletin board.

Brag it up!
Talk about an achievement or personal quality of a family member to someone else. Do this within earshot of the person, or to someone who may repeat the compliment. A compliment is always greater when it is delivered second hand.

Play the Family Survivor Game
Gather the family in the living room or around the dinner table and ask each person to make a list of the strengths of each family member which would help all of you survive when stranded on a deserted island. Encourage both serious and funny entries.

Example:

Mom could sew all our clothes when they wore out.

Dad would build a boat and get us out of there.

Bonnie would sing for us and entertain us in the evenings with jokes.

Carl knows a lot about first-aid and would bandage our wounds.

Older family members may get more outrageous:

Mike wouldn't waste his science degree even on a deserted island. He would figure out a way to make rum so we could barter with pirates to get us off the island!

OPPORTUNITYISNOWHERE

What did you read when you first looked at these words? Put these letters up on a banner and ask your family to read it out loud simultaneously. You will hear some of them read it as, "Opportunity is NO WHERE," while others will say, "Opportunity is NOW HERE." This is an eye-opening activity to start a discussion on how we look at situations and approach obstacles and opportunities in life.

When doing this activity, the letters must be very uniform in size and spacing. It is best if you can type out the letters and blow them up on your computer or photocopier. Also, don't give them time to study the words or see them in advance. Rather, uncover or hold up the sign and ask them to read it immediately.

Building a Solid Work Ethic

*The greatest good you can do for another is not just to share
your riches but to reveal to him his own.*
~ Benjamin Disraeli

Valuable Lessons

We had a problem, and it was becoming more evident by the moment. Our oldest daughter, Sandy, wanted to attend our church's youth group retreat, and the benefits of her going were becoming very clear as she laid out all the details for our consideration. An excellent proponent for her case, she formed an airtight argument full of all the parent trappings one would expect. It would be well chaperoned, it was for a good purpose, and *everyone* else was going.

One piece she forgot in her proposition was the amount of money this trip would cost. Money, dinero, cash, the green stuff that makes the world go around. She didn't really want to discuss the cost of the trip, but when, within an hour of our discussion, the phone rang and it was the neighbor calling to hire Sandy for some babysitting and offering to pay her *money* and Sandy turned her down, I realized there was a real disconnect between earning money and wanting special things.

Let me be frank, it was a great opportunity and we could afford the cost of the camp. It wasn't about the expenditure; it was about the realization that we had not adequately taught our children the value of money. Immediately we put our heads together and developed a plan to expand the fiscal awareness of our children. The following Sunday evening we called our regular family meeting around the breakfast room table and made a few eye-popping announcements.

"Effective immediately, we are cancelling all allowances for the oldest three children. Wendy is still young, and will therefore keep hers until she is twelve." The looks on their faces were of total shock and dismay, as you might expect. This was a monetary crisis like they had never faced before.

"Instead, we are going to start matching funds." Curiosity returned to their faces and I recognized the look of hope—the hope that whatever this new plan was, it would include the flow of currency through their hands.

My wife, Velda, gave each of them a small notebook in which she had already drawn columns and made headings for tracking their earnings, savings, and giving.

"Here is how the new system works," I explained. "For every dollar you earn on your own, we will match you dollar for dollar. All you have to do is keep a record of your earnings, savings, and giving in this notebook." The designated amount was ten percent for savings and another ten percent for charitable giving.

It was amazing how their attitudes about looking for and accepting jobs changed. Children love the independent feeling of making money, and it was no shock to find out that my children were babysitting tycoons and lawn mowing financiers. The system was working and they were highly motivated to double their incomes.

We continued our matching funds system up through high school, which was a large boost to their independent solvency. As they earned larger sums of money, we reduced the number of items we purchased for them. In time they became responsible for purchasing all their own clothes and personal items for the purpose of teaching them to respect the value of a dollar.

What good comes from parents who always step up behind their children with wallets open, ready to pay bail on whatever the item is they have their eyes on? That system teaches them to be dependent, to act on whims and to expect entitlements. Matching funds teaches young people to manage their own spending habits and develop their own earning potential.

I marveled at their entrepreneurship and their grasp of finances. My son, Steve, started his own business as a shoe shiner at a local barbershop when he was in the seventh grade and I had the privilege of making his first business loan to purchase all the professional supplies he would need. His reputation of being a hard worker spread to a nearby business and eventually he added janitorial services for the next-door print shop to his list of clients. I had business cards printed for Steve and even hired him to clean my business office.

Other families have used various means of teaching their children about money and many of them are very good. It is important to have a plan that you stick with, and to be purposeful about teaching the next generation about the value of a dollar.

Diligent, honest, and productive work is the backbone of a strong family and nation.

Dad's Work Ethic

Work consists of whatever a body is obliged to do,
and play consists of whatever a body is not obliged to do.
~ Mark Twain, *The Adventures of Tom Sawyer*

Things have changed a lot since the time of my first job. At the age of fourteen, I was paid seventy-five cents per hour and allowed to work as a construction helper where my dad was the director of horticulture for the parks department. Today you can't hire a kid that young because of liabilities, and when they are old enough, the starting wage is much higher to satisfy the state's minimum wage requirement. One thing that has not changed over the years, however, is the value of a strong work ethic.

Working in a place where my dad was the "boss" afforded me no extra privileges. In fact, I quickly realized that working for my dad meant being assigned to the least attractive jobs and being expected to take them on with a good work ethic and enthusiasm.

My dad was a hard worker and expected me to follow suit. Although my primary duty that first summer of full time work was to assist in building the greenhouse, my task every Monday was to walk through the main park campus with a gunnysack slung over my shoulder and a walking stick with a nail attached to the end and pick up any paper, bottles, or trash left behind by the public. Not the most inspiring job for a lad of my age, but that first day did afford me a memorable learning experience.

Dad met me with his pickup truck at a prearranged point and we backtracked over my route, picking up the garbage sacks I had deposited along the way. He then drove to the entrance of the park and stopped where we had a wide sweeping view of the area. He said, "Do you see that piece of paper over there? And that bottle over there? Your mother is not going to come along after you and pick them up; you are being paid to do this job. Now go back and make sure you have covered everything thoroughly!"

What a great and painful lesson on the importance of doing a job thoroughly. His words still ring in my ears sixty-two years later when I am in the midst of a task.

Every person is responsible for taking care of something. I was Ruler Over the Garbage but didn't see the significance of that role at first. The lesson I took from that day is that it doesn't matter how large or small the job, whether you think this is a career builder, or if the money is good or lousy. Every job is a career builder because every job has your signature on it and the quality you put out is telling someone else how much you can be relied upon with the bigger things. In every job, show yourself to be trustworthy with the little things, then your boss will know you are worthy of the bigger things.

Heave-Ho! – Family Working Together

I'm always game for a new adventure, especially one that includes the opportunity to roll up our sleeves and get dirty together. When our family took trips out to Camp Harmony to put on a recreational family camp, there was always abounding opportunity for adventure, wonder, barrier breakers, and exhaustion. I'm talking about the good kind of exhaustion that makes your body tingle and pulse, followed by a bit of good recovery time and a feeling of satisfaction.

Each trip took the cooperative efforts of each and every person to do prep work, load the gear, unload the boats and haul everything out to the camp sites to set up the cooking station and activities. Lifting, running, and working together caused most of us to break a sweat and break down walls of separation. Working together brought us together.

Even the youngest were given tasks to accomplish where they would rub shoulders with their older cousins, aunts, uncles, grandparents, and friends. All in an effort for them to learn there is something each one of us can contribute. Team work strengthens the family. Working together, accomplishing something worthwhile, building memories and just being together. It was always satisfying.

It doesn't really matter what we are doing or accomplishing, it is more about the fact that we are all spending time together working toward a common end. I have decided a pretty good idea is for me to create opportunities for everyone to come together on these projects and then get out of their way! These kids have such enthusiasm for the undertaking and far more inborn ingenuity for accomplishing tasks than I do.

As a group of grandkids sat reminiscing about Camp Harmony, my grandson Jason had this to say: *"The thing that made Camp Harmony so unique was how our family had to work together and incorporate the other people who were there as well. We had to take a task like carrying all the gear up to the top of a hill and we had to figure out how to do that together. It really broke down barriers and made us a lot closer."*

"Doing" Together

Recently my wife and I purchased the property adjacent to our home. Canopied by tall old trees and carpeted with lush ground covering, with a rustic old house nestled in the middle, the property was the ideal campground and gathering place for our family. What some would have seen as a complete tear-down, we saw as a prime spot for building family memories. Having a place where we can all convene for gatherings over the years was purpose enough to put some "heave-ho" into this property. Sleeves up, we wasted no time jumping on the task of bringing this land, and the old house, up to more modern standards.

The grand unveiling of this property brought more enthusiasm than even I was expecting, especially among the older grandsons, who quickly started putting their heads together over how the property could be improved and when we could get started with our first work party.

It warms my heart to see their enthusiasm and to see how that spirit is spread right down to the youngest generations. The youngest may only carry a few sticks over to the fire. The important lesson is that they are helping too, and we are all building a legacy together. It is more about the act of *building* and *doing* together than the final outcome itself. We want to see these younger generations keep this family spirit going for multiple generations beyond them. These types of investments and projects are just tools to help them along that journey.

One day I was talking on the phone with one of my grandsons who was planning to come out and do some work on the place mid-week. He had the extra time and I sure needed help getting things ready for our annual Grandkid Weekend. We talked through the project and how I would make sure all the supplies where there and how much I appreciated his involvement. Before hanging up the phone he had one last question for me, "Are you going to be there to work with me, Grandpa?" That's what mattered. Were we going to be able to spend some time together on this project? It really doesn't matter what we accomplish, it is all about the fact that we are "doing" together and "doing" is the linchpin of healthy growing family relationships.

Outward

Outward focus is the byproduct of a healthy family. When we know we have been blessed we are able to turn to our community with acts of service. The fulfillment and life lessons that come from helping others are some of the richest rewards we can receive in life.

One of my granddaughters tells this moving story about an activity her father set up for her and her two older sisters on a Daughters Day out with Dad.

"After lunch our dad gave each of us a shopping list with random items on it and told us that we had a combined budget of $500 and 30 minutes to find as many items as we could on the list, pay for them, and get them to the car. We had no idea why, but the whole thing seemed like fun and we were game! You should have seen the three of us throwing stuff into our carts and running up and down the aisles! We left the store with the car fully loaded up and still wondering what this was all about. Dad drove us to the Friendship House, a homeless shelter, and we delivered all these purchases to them. We got to visit with the people there and learn about more of their needs. It was an amazing experience."

Do you know how good it feels to a child when they are given the chance to help someone else with a true need? It shapes them. This is a key component in raising a balanced family. We build a strong core with so much heart that it is natural to turn it outward into service and stewardship to others. It is one of the most impacting experiences they will ever have and will shape the people they grow into.

Routinely take part in random acts of kindness and service with your family:

- Volunteer at a food bank.
- Help a neighbor, community center, or church with a project.
- Take a meal to someone who is ill or going through a rough time.
- Stop to talk to someone who looks lonely.
- Help raise money for an organization that serves people in need.
- With humility, allow your children to know when you donate to a charity.

- Sponsor a child in an impoverished country and have your children write letters to that child.

Family Work Parties

A parent or grandparent is a lot like the coach of a sports team in that sometimes the most important part of our job is making a plan and calling the plays so that others have a chance to come together and utilize their gifts and talents.

Some years ago we called up the adult kids and suggested we schedule a family work day at each of their homes. We would choose dates that worked best for everyone and we would all show up with whatever tools, head knowledge, and energy we needed to accomplish a few tasks as a group. This really took a huge project that may be rather daunting for one family to handle and turned it into a fun family gathering where everyone was needed and appreciated.

We put up fences, painted buildings, took out shrubs, and fixed plumbing. Everyone showed up, if it was at all possible, because there was something that everyone could have a hand in, no matter their age or ability level.

What this amounts to is the spirit of a good old-fashioned barn raising party. It could be cleaning out an attic to prepare for a garage sale, landscaping the back yard, or a deep cleaning with a few painting projects. Many hands make light work and I will guarantee you that bringing the family together to serve one another with generous acts of kindness will leave everyone feeling loved and fulfilled. This spirit of generosity will spread like wildfire to the youngsters who are soaking in the spirit of a family working together.

Everyone has a hand in it. Grandma might want to bring some snacks and lemonade to keep everyone's energy up during the day, and the littlest ones may be commissioned to work alongside Dad and a favorite uncle to run and fetch tools or carry twigs to the fire. Maybe there is a family member who never seems to feel like he or she has much to offer; this day just may be the perfect setting for that person to shine by applying certain skills or knowledge that are not often called upon.

Something magical happens when you give service and sweat together.

Caught it!

Growing up in a family greenhouse business meant a 24-hour-a-day, seven-day-a-week job, 365 days out of the year for all members of the family. Certain tasks just couldn't be ignored or left for another day. Working alongside Dad and other family members, I didn't really understand the early lessons I was learning about values and work ethic; I now know it was dripping into me with life-impacting persistence.

Like any grade school child, I grumbled about the tasks that were assigned to me: stacking wood, cutting kindling, weeding, and watering. But working alongside other family members showed me that this was the norm. At a deeper level I understood that, even though I would have rather been playing games with my buddies, work was good for me, and as the youngest member of my family, I wanted to prove my value to the family team.

At the time, I didn't comprehend that these lessons would become an important part of my value system and that eventually I would press them into my children who would then pass them along to their own families. But it happened, and the generational link is priceless.

Realizing the wedding anniversary of my oldest daughter, Sandy, and her husband Bill, was going to piggy-back another family gathering, I decided to contact their children to see if I could offer our house as a location to celebrate their parents. I sent a text to all four grandchildren at around 7:00 pm asking them to call me. Often this is how I contact them because I know they all have busy lives and families of their own, and I prefer to just have them call me when they are free if the matter isn't urgent. The first return call came at 9:00 pm that evening from a granddaughter apologizing for not getting back to me sooner as she had been participating in a company event that evening. The other three returned the call the next day, each explaining they had been busy when I texted them. One was presenting for a city council meeting, another was attending a school board meeting, and one was teaching an exercise class. It was evident the family work ethic had been caught; these adult grandchildren are fully engaged in their communities and careers. This is the goal.

Work is good and should be approached with vigor and an attitude of value for what is accomplished both physically and relationally. We were created to work and, as adults in our families, we will do a great service to our children and grandchildren if we model high standards and esteem for all work-centered contributions.

The Earl of Derby said it well when he addressed the pupils of Liverpool College, saying, "The vast majority of men, in all ages and countries, must work before they can eat. Even those who are not under the necessity, are. . . to adopt what is called an active pursuit of some sort. . . every member of a community is bound to do something for that community, in return for what he gets from it."

Do all the good you can, by all the means you can,
in all the ways you can, in all the places you can,
at all the times you can, to all the people you can, as long as you can.
~ Commonly attributed to John Wesley

Anchor Points

Teach Money Management

Develop a system to help your children earn money. Teach them how to save, donate and spend appropriately.

- Matching Funds

  Set up a system to reward your children for working independently. In our family we offered a dollar-for-dollar matching system, but each family needs to set up workable guidelines that may include certain limits enabling the parent to keep up with the arrangement. Maybe offering an additional fifty cents for every dollar or matching funds up to a certain dollar amount would work better for some families.

  As the financial base is increased for the child, the parent should begin having the child budget for certain necessity items like clothing, entertainment, gifts, and lunches.

- Family Job Board

  Some families will post a job with the specifications for completion along with the amount of money paid for a job well done. The children are allowed to look over the job board and claim a task for the opportunity to roll up their sleeves and earn some spending cash.

  Examples:

  Wanted: Chief Hedge Clipper
  Task Includes: Trim the hedge against Mr. Jones fence down to the top of the fence line. Pick up all debris and place it in the burn pile. Replace all tools in garage. Must be completed by Saturday afternoon.
  Pay: $10

Wanted: Car Detailer
Task Includes: Wash Mom's car. Vacuum the inside and apply leather conditioner to the seats.
Pay: $12

Wanted: Window Washer
Task Includes: Wash all the windows on the front of the house, inside and out.
Pay: $6, with a $2 bonus if you whistle while you work!

Note: Children should have certain chores which they are expected to do as a member of the family. For instance, do not pay a child for making his own bed, washing dishes or feeding the pets. The paid jobs should be over and above daily chores.

Expose Children to Your Work

Take your children to work with you from time to time. This exposure allows them to gain an understanding of what you do and they will learn from the example of seeing tasks accomplished, business etiquette, professional relationships, and the necessity of work in our society. Demonstrate that work is good and it is rewarding.

Seek and Serve

At a family meeting, discuss how your family might be able to offer some work on a task for a person in need. For example, an elderly neighbor may need some help stacking firewood, or a family member with a new baby would feel blessed if we were to drop off dinner and spend time helping with weeding the flower beds.

Get them Thinking

- Ask probing questions to get younger children thinking: What would happen if everyone stopped working?
- What if the mail man stopped working, or the farmer, police, president, or any person relevant to that child?
- Include family members: What if dad stopped working? What if mom stopped all the work she does around the house or if you stopped doing your chores? What would things be like?

Show Genuine Interest

Show interest in the work that each member of your family does. Ask about their occupation and communicate how you value what they do. This is effective with all ages, from the youngest paper boy all the way up to the oldest business executive.

Throw a Work Party

- Set up a Family Work Party Calendar. Ask each grown family member to communicate back to you a project at their house they would like help with. Attempt to find the most workable dates possible for everyone and notify everyone of those dates well in advance to insure a higher level of availability.
- Be understanding when there are times certain members are not able to attend. The purpose is to develop family teamwork. Giving someone a scowl or lecture about not participating is counterproductive.
- Send a memo to each family member with the dates and tasks for each work party.

- Make a phone call or send a message to each family member a few days before the date, reminding them that we are all getting together and how great it will be. Make the memo funny, and complimentary:

Example:

Hi Everyone,

Just a reminder this is Wrecking Ball Weekend! We will be tearing down the old shed at Dave and Phyllis' house. All levels of brain and brawn are needed. The ladies have plans for some good food after the project.

Sure appreciate how you all help out with these work days. You are a blessing!

Dad and Mom

- Make it sound like a lot of fun. Include plans for snacks or meals.
- Rest after the job is done: If time allows, plan to stick around and rest together after the task is finished. This is an important time of reflection and renewal while the family connects through conversation, and maybe even the mending of a few sore muscles.
- Show gratitude: Send a follow-up message to everyone thanking them for participating. Ideally, the family that received the work party will do this as well.
- Don't overwhelm everyone by planning too many of these work days.

Volunteer in Your Community

Suggest that your family volunteers together for a community event:

- Volunteer at the food bank, soup kitchen or favorite charity
- Participate in a bike-a-thon together
- Plant trees in a city park
- Play music, read books or play games with elderly residence at a grandparent's retirement home.

The elevator to success is not running; you must climb the stairs.
~ Zig Ziglar

Success is a ladder you cannot climb with your hands in your pockets.
~ American Proverb

The one who is unwilling to work shall not eat.
~ 2 Thessalonians 3:10

Refined by Mentors

Don't worry that children never listen to you.
Worry that they are always watching you.
~ Robert Fulghum

Caught Not Taught

Which American company has its finger on the pulse of young people more than Coca-Cola®? Since the late 1800s, this company has been on the leading edge of advertising with its slogan aimed at one of our deepest values. *"It's the Real Thing, Baby"* is the benchmark slogan for Coke, and this truism permeated itself into an American maxim. Not just for love of the carbonated concoction, but for our deeper love of things that are real, genuine, and authentic.

In our children's eyes, we must be the real thing, baby. They are constantly watching how we interact and the choices we make. If our words don't line up with our actions, we are doomed. This is the "show me, don't tell me" generation, and influencing them means first making it a priority to connect with them. The younger members of our families want real relationships with real people who set examples worthy of catching.

Anxious to understand more about spreading positive influence to my family, I looked up the definition of the word "contagious" through dictionary.com and found: *Capable of being transmitted or spread from one person to another by direct or indirect contact. Synonym – Infectious.*

Everything about us is contagious, for the better or the worse, and will surface in our words, actions, and entire approach to life. An influential parent or grandparent will make sure the habits of their life are worth catching.

Realistically, it is impossible for a parent, grandparent, aunt or uncle to avoid being role models. The thought that the way we live has zero affect on our posterity is completely unreasonable. Our children are watching us and absorbing our actions and attitudes all the time. It takes effort, and there will be mistakes along the way, but our goal should be to live a life defined by high moral values, vibrant relationships, active lifestyles, humility and generosity. This cuts a clear and inviting path for our children to follow.

I remember in the past, certain sports stars who made large public moral blunders, followed them up with announcements that they did not feel their actions warranted the public fury over their poor example to their young fans. A couple of them made statements proclaiming, "I never said I wanted to be a role model." Nonsense! When the eyes of the younger generation are on you, you *are* a role model and, with a bit of self-control and purposeful living, it can be a rewarding role to play.

Some of my greatest lessons in life were not taught to me, but instead were caught through observation of good role models. The way I learned to treat my parents with respect came from watching the way they treated *their* parents with respect. Even when my father disagreed with my mom's parents on an issue, he would still treat them with respect. Mom and Dad never stated these behaviors as rules, but displayed them as unwavering values, which were admired and carried on by my siblings and me. Shadowing my parents, I learned how to pray, how to work, and how to love my family.

Whether the example is positive or negative, it is still being observed as a pattern for the way to live. This should raise our awareness of the importance of selecting the type of people we allow to have the greatest influence on our children. Example is the cornerstone of influence and should be handled particularly thoughtfully. When Albert Schweitzer was asked how to raise children, he answered, "Three principles: first, example; second, example; third, example."

Clearly, parents are the first and foremost examples in their children's lives, and because of that, we all need to have a "look-in-the-mirror moment" and ask if we possess that which we want to pass along to our children. I can't expect my kids to pick up qualities which are nonexistent in me. By first investing in the development of their own strengths, parents will become effective at guiding their children. This growth comes through developing positive associations, reading good books, and being more aware of your role as a model. Character isn't something you mandate; it is something you model.

The way we spend our time, the integrity we display, the words we speak, and the values we live out, all influence our children's perspective on life and will, in turn, be lived out in their own lives. This is a bit like gravity, it is not a principle formulated through fancy research; it is more like an undeniable natural law.

Someone will be a mentor to our children. If we don't expand their circle of influence with quality role models and build our relationship with them, they will find it in someone else, for better or worse.

Positive Areas to Model

- Put others up (speak well of others and give words of encouragement liberally)
- Be a loyal friend
- Attend church
- Be a person of high integrity
- Give service to others
- Pray
- Read good books
- Be punctual
- Demonstrate a strong work ethic
- Be respectful to others
- Do what you say you are going to do
- Live by the Golden Rule (Treat others the way you would want them to treat you.)

Inviting Role Models into Your Lives

Tell me and I forget, teach me and I may remember,
involve me and I will learn.
~ Benjamin Franklin

If you don't want your children going through the school of hard knocks, set them up with mentors who will take them through the school of wisdom and strong council. In a practical sense, we have a lot of power to decide with whom we go through life and whom we will invite to influence our children. Those people in positions of influence should be mature and always guiding with a strong moral compass.

Now think about this: If our young people spend most of their time developing their outlook with only the limited perspective of their peers, it will be nearly impossible to develop confidence, skills, and momentum for the life ahead of them. "Peer think" doesn't develop children; relationships with vibrant role models do.

At different times, when our family was young, we would invite people whom we felt would have a positive impact on our children to come spend time in our home or accompany us on family outings. Occasionally, we were able to offer a longer-term stay for the purpose of providing temporary housing to someone who would rub some good stuff off on our young and impressionable children. A number of our grandchildren have commented to their parents, "Gee, you have a lot of older friends." That is very true, because many of these mentors who were introduced into their lives as young to middle-aged adults have stayed in their social circle and continue to be a positive influence in their network of people.

Since education is something our family has always highly valued, we have regularly sought out inspiring, academically-oriented people to be guests in our home. On one of these occasions, we opened our home to a college student working on his Ph.D. Another time it was a married couple, where the husband, Dr. Larry, was finishing his residency to become a surgeon. These young, energetic, goal-focused students had positive attributes just flowing out of them, and I was grateful to be able to put my children in a position to benefit from these outstanding role models.

Interactions with these role models need not be over-worked or too planned out. Casual conversations and weekend activities provided ample opportunity for our children to soak up the overflow of good substance from these young adults. Good role models send messages about their values by what they naturally do and say. Just get the right people in the same room or on the same outing as your family, and you will see the impact it has.

Staying connected with high-caliber people is key. One of the professionals who had stayed in our home became the Director of the Heart Research Center at OHSU in Portland, Oregon. Years after his stay with our family I was able to call and ask him for a personal tour of his department for our adult children and their spouses.

We included this tour during what we call Mystery Weekend, an annual event for our adult children and spouses to get away with us and spend quality time together. The kids never know the activities that we plan for them during these weekends, but we often try to include an educational or inspiring opportunity. On this occasion, all of our eyes were popping as we learned about the cutting-edge technologies now available to heart patients. It was especially inspiring to hear it from someone who had made such a strong impression on our children during his college days.

I guess you could call me a collector of people. Even if it means putting myself outside my personal comfort zone to gain a new relationship that I feel will be valuable, I'll do it. Often I'll ask friends to help connect me with interesting and influential people in their circles. Other times, I'll just make a few inquiring phone calls and have been surprised by the willingness on the other end. Realize that the best compliment you can pay to another person is to ask them to come and assist you in being a mentor for yourself and your children.

Exposure to people who had knowledge, experience and expertise that we did not have within our own home was always our goal. I am just a businessman and a family man, but through association, I have been able to introduce my family to authors, professors, presidents, CEOs, doctors, professional athletes, television personalities, missionaries, scientists, and world speakers.

Through association with people like this, our children grow in their own self-esteem and become comfortable interacting with highly successful and even well-known figures. They won't be fearful or intimidated by people who are prominent. Instead, they will view them as normal folks, because they have had the opportunity to have intriguing dinner conversations, attend business parties, go boating, or camping and have even had a few interesting individuals spend the night and sit with them at their own breakfast table the next morning. At first these people are mentors, but through relationship they become their friends and their network of influence in their adult life.

As iron sharpens iron, so one man sharpens another.
~ Proverbs 27:17

Social Skills and Good Manners

Train a child in the way he should go and
when he is old he will not depart from it.
~ Proverbs 22:6

Every time we took our children into uncharted territory, whether it was entertaining a guest in our home or attending a business meeting in a five-star hotel, we prepared them for the social graces they would need to put into practice. Making sure they were well-instructed in advance meant they would approach the situation with more confidence, and in return, they received praise and respect from those adults. Even though they are now independent adults, our children will look to us with questions about protocol for certain situations. This practical training is a life skill which we adults are responsible for passing onto our children, and the training starts at a very young age.

Good manners are not a natural part of our DNA, and without some deliberate training by the adults at home, the younger generation will come up short when placed in important social and business settings. It doesn't matter how laid-back society tries to become, good manners and social graces are still respected and carry a person a long way. The fact is, most business people do appreciate good manners, and when a hiring opportunity arises, they will look for an employee with well-practiced social skills and decorum. Have you prepared your family in this way? The bonus is that families who use good manners routinely at home tend to be high functioning and experience reduced conflict.

Essentials to Model and Teach

Dress Properly for the Occasion

Dress with care and appropriateness for each situation. The way you dress shows the level of importance you give to the event. Sure, a person may feel more comfortable in an old pair of blue jeans and T-shirt, but the employer, scholarship committee, judge, or bride may not feel too complimented by the lack of effort. Neat and clean always wins.

Shake Hands and Make Eye Contact

Even the youngest of children should be taught to make eye contact and offer their hand for a firm handshake. The young person who is taught to offer this gesture first will gain the respect of adults. They will be at ease with such social graces when they are older.

Use "Please," "Thank you," and "You're welcome"

Simple but powerful. We should all model these habits routinely in conversations and remind young people to do so as well.

Serve Others

Whether it is in your own home or in public settings, make service to others your routine. "May I take your coat?" "Would you like a glass of water?" "Let me carry your bags..."

Open the Door for Others

Contrary to popular myth, this is not a chauvinistic practice. Considerate people hold the door open for their peers, their mother, their dad, and strangers. They also step aside to let others pass and hold the elevator for late comers. Good manners always say, "After you."

Stand Up When an Elder Enters the Room

Too many have forgotten this prized symbol of respect. No matter what age you are, always stand to greet grandparents, aunts, uncles, teachers, and special guests.

Send Thank-you Notes

Teach young people the power of gratitude in action. It is one thing to say "thank you" for a gift or invitation to a special occasion; it is a whole different ball game when one picks up the habit of putting pen to paper. Develop the polished habit of being known as someone who sends inked thank-you notes. It doesn't have to be elaborate, just make it sincere.

Be Polite to People Who Serve You

This means make eye contact, smile and speak to the person behind the counter. Turn your phone off when talking to the cashier at the gas station or at the grocery store. Be respectful to the server at the restaurant and say, "Thank you" when you're given food or change. Try thanking the bus driver for the ride home or a soldier for serving our country.

Always Be on Time

Plan to leave the house early enough to allow for traffic slowdowns and other unexpected delays. Being "fashionably late" is an arrogant myth. We show respect for others when we are prompt. If, on a rare occasion, you are running late, use that phone in your pocket to make a courtesy call and let them know what happened.

Start Conversations

Teach young people the importance of striking up conversation. It shows that you value the other person's presence enough to engage them. Ask, "How are you?" "Where are you coming from today?" "Do you have plans for the weekend?" "What's new with your family?" "Did you grow up around here?" "What did you think of (the speaker, the weather, a current event, etc.)?" Ask questions that show interest.

Use Good Table Manners

The family dinner table is one of the best venues for teaching social graces. Model and remind them that this is a specific time to arrive cleaned up, engage in conversation, use good posture, and eat with your mouth closed. Don't allow grabbing and teach consideration of portions so there is enough for everyone. "Would you please pass the potatoes?" "Can I pour more water for you?" "Thank you for the nice meal." "May I be excused?" Teaching proper use of utensils and how to eat politely will save your child from unnecessary embarrassment at some point in life.

Teaching these habits from a young age is ideal, but if you are just now becoming aware of these little gems of success, start today at whatever age your children currently are. You want your family to receive the natural benefits that come from graciously and instinctively using these habits. A mutual sense of satisfaction is evident between people who interact with respect. A natural result is that more doors open and more opportunities will be given to those who care enough about others to polish up on these habits.

The hardest job kids face today is learning
good manners without seeing any.
~ Fred Astaire

Networking for Your Family

It's hard to miss the headlines that remind us daily of how the American financial system has been experiencing the greatest economic disaster since the Great Depression. It was inevitable that this global crisis would hit home in my own family. Indeed it did, with especially heavy effects for one of our grandsons. As he lost his footing financially during this great recession, it caused me to start looking into how certain members of our own family might be able to come around him, help him regain his self-esteem, and find a worthy job.

I picked up the phone and called a few of the other men in our family, explaining the situation to them and how I felt each of them had perspective, insight and key connections to help this family member find a job and gain some confidence. It's interesting how these roles change. It used to be my contact list that carried the most bang for networking; now I'm calling on my children and grandchildren to make connections through their networks. A family that understands and nurtures good relationships will find these networks to be quite powerful in business and personal relations.

All the men I called understood the situation and were eager to be a part of the solution. Like being called into a military strategy room, we cleared our schedules and started meeting on Saturday mornings in the office of my son-in-law who had access to a computer and online job listings.

Coffee cups gripped firmly in our hands, we were on a mission and everyone brought valuable ideas to the table. Cooperatively employing our insider resources, experience and knowledge, we set out to prepare this family member for a new beginning with a stable job. Nothing is worse than looking for a job on your own and coming up short. This support group was going to keep focused and moving forward until our mission was accomplished.

The *aha!* moment came when we realized that this men's group was not only about finding a job for one member; we had become a reciprocating support group. An accountability group really, and exceptional things were bubbling out of it. Soon we were not just focused on the needs of one member, but the confluence of all the members dialoguing and pouring into the greater whole. Each person's strengths showed us we all had something to gain.

Together we started working through a book called *Strengths Finder*, by Tom Rath. Each one of us took online tests to find our personal strengths. We have greatly benefited from gaining more understanding of those strengths and how they will help us individually and as a family. Learning about one another's strengths in this group setting really boosted our relationships with each other, as well as our careers. Many of us keep in contact during the week by exchanging encouraging emails. It all works together and keeps everyone rolling in the right direction.

There is an interconnectedness among members that bonds the family, much like mountain climbers who rope themselves together when climbing a mountain, so that if someone should slip or need support, he's held up by the others until he regains his footing.
~ Phil McGraw, Family First

No Man is an Island

Over the next five years, the people you meet and
the books you read will determine the person you will become.
~ Charlie Jones

In the previous story, did you happen to notice how much work I did in order to accomplish such a large goal? I made a few phone calls to the right people and I showed up. That's all. It's about being the person who is willing to take initiative and gets the ball rolling. No man is an island; we need the strengths of our family, and families need a larger network of mentors and relationships beyond themselves. Those relationships should include people of all social, educational, and economic strata. Diverse associations will develop our children into more interesting people with greater perspective, savvy and sensitivity as they are immersed in rich exposure through other people's stories and experiences.

My good friend and personal mentor, Ted Engstrom, was the president of World Vision in the 1980s and '90s. In a position like his, he knew a lot about networking people of varied backgrounds and strengths. Ted always told me, "Everyone needs a Barnabas and a Timothy." In other words, everyone needs someone to be mentored by and someone else to mentor. At any age, we can learn something from everyone, and we can give something as well.

This bridging together of diverse relationships will educate your family and allow them to build worthy relationships, which they may draw from in the future.

When I stand before God at the end of my life, I would hope
that I would not have a single bit of talent left,
and could say, "I used everything you gave me."
~ Erma Bombeck

What Will the Neighbors Think?

Have you had much experience with people of different backgrounds than your own? How about interactions with folks of different racial, economic, religious, and educational backgrounds? Most of us stick to people who are very similar to ourselves, but believe me when I say that exposing your family to a diverse group of people will give them valuable perspective and greater people skills. We are not only formed by our interactions with people of strong business and academic backgrounds, we are equally formed through involvement with people who are quite dissimilar from ourselves and our own experiences.

In the mid 1960s, our family lived in an upper-middle-class neighborhood in Seattle, Washington. At that time, racial discrimination was overt throughout the country, and we lived in a particularly white neighborhood where any minority person was met with distrust. I wasn't about to become a part of this racial-class mayhem and, in fact, made it a purpose to counter the bias of the day by inviting multi-cultural visitors into our home. It was important to me that our family be entirely at ease with people of other ethnicities and that our children did not develop any prejudice toward them.

A front yard visit with my neighbor was a pleasant routine in our part of the city. However, against the backdrop of prejudice, the normal niceties were about to become a dicey presupposition on my neighbor's part when a black friend of mine stopped by for a visit.

Looking past me, through a narrowed brow, at the car and driver pulling up in front of my house, my neighbor asked, "What is that _____ doing here?" With a pleased lilt in my voice, I said, "He is a friend of mine." I turned on my heels and walked over to greet him.

I suppose I brought another shock wave to the old neighborhood when my college friend, Fred Newkirk, who runs an inner city ministry in Long Beach, California, called to see if we would be willing to host a bunch of these kids at our house for a few days and take them out on our boat. "Sure!" I said, anticipating what a magnificent chance this would be for my kids to host other kids from a completely different life experience.

Finally, the long-awaited day arrived, and a van full of kids pulled into the drive. Most were African-American, and since we lived in an entirely white neighborhood, I welcomed the opportunity for my kids to engage with these young people. I wanted our children to become comfortable relating to kids of a different race. Our new friends seemed to enjoy looking around the house and enjoyed the environment.

When it was time to head out to the boat, we noticed that one of the girls was missing. The leader set out to find her, and when he did, he came back to me and tenderly explained where he had found her. This young girl, without a home and personal items of her very own, had nestled herself in my daughter's bedroom. She only wanted to be alone and to enjoy the comforts of a private bedroom. Just once. Even though the boat ride was the most exciting activity for most of the others, this young girl just wanted permission to hang out in the bedroom by herself—to be alone and have her very own space. What a new perspective this was for my own children.

Seeking out diverse people and opportunities for our family has been an interesting pastime. We have entertained presidents and trustees of universities, successful business people, missionaries, authors, speakers, a couple of celebrities, affluent people, and truly underprivileged people, all because it is important to know and accept folks of all walks of life.

Anchor Points

Invite Interesting People into Your Life

Make a point of inviting someone of interest to have dinner in your home or to participate in an activity with your family on a regular basis. Once a month would be a good start. Start with a list of people who fit into different categories of interest to your family:

Traveler	Artist	Musician
Educator	Soldier	Missionary
Interesting Career	Unique Hobby	

Encourage Table Talk

Come to the table ready to ask questions and share some thought-provoking ideas. Current events, inspiring stories, and probing questions keep family interactions lively and something to look forward to. Keep it light and genuine. Humor is always a winner and reading a short portion from a humorous or critical editorial can stir up some great table talk. There may be some contemporary editorials out there which may work well, but I think Dave Barry, Erma Bombeck, and Paul Harvey stand the test of time.

Make sure you are not so prepared that the family feels they are sitting down for a nightly lecture. Engage them in the conversations and capture their interest. Listen to their thoughts.

Key talking points:
- Ask about school/education:
  o How is school?
  o What interests you most in school?

- o What are your plans and goals for your education?
- o Is there anything I can do to help you?

- Ask questions about things on which they can educate you:
  - o Can you show me how to use more functions on my cell phone?
  - o Can you tell me about texting?
  - o Is this how you would like me to connect with you?
  - o How does Twitter work?
  - o Do you ever Skype or use other forms of video conferencing? Ask how it works and suggest chatting with a relative that lives a distance away.
- Ask thoughtful questions:
  - o Where do you see yourself and what would you like to be doing in five years?
  - o What are you doing to prepare yourself to get there?
  - o What can I do to help you get there?
  - o What do you wish we, as a family, did more?
  - o What would you like to change about our family? Be vulnerable.
  - o What is your favorite movie, book, magazine, website? Ask questions about those items and find out what it is they like about the story line, or genre.
- Think ahead to ask good questions or to offer interesting information based on the other person's interests.

Read Books

For the younger children, give them strong doses of inspiration by reading to them books about courage, honor and leadership. Give books as gifts to your older adult children to keep them growing.

YWAM Publishing (Youth with a Mission) offers a large selection of books on these topics, as do many other publishers

Model reading to your family by always having a good book in process. Share interesting information from the book with your family.

Participate in Small Groups

Beginning during the teenage years and carrying through adulthood, encourage each family member to take part in a small accountability group with interesting and high quality people. This could be a study group, think tank, networking group, or hobby group.

Being involved with a larger circle of influence is excellent for personal development. Take the initiative to get one of these groups started if there is not one for you to join.

Find a Cause or Outreach

Look to the needs of your community and get the family involved in service. Homeless shelters, food banks, churches, and the like all benefit from volunteer hours. Model reaching out to others.

Ask Probing Questions

Get the family to share their thoughts and ideas:

- I was reading in the paper today that our mayor is considering. . . "What are your thoughts regarding this issue?"
- Read one of Aesop's Fables or other short story with a moral- or values-based message. After reading out loud to your family, start a discussion about the points of the story.
- Tell the family about a current event and get them involved in a discussion on the topic.

- Ask an intriguing question at the breakfast table or before you leave for work. Something like, "Did you know_____?" Then leave them hanging with, "We'll talk about it at dinner tonight." Be sure that you remember to finish the conversation at dinner.

Interview an Accomplished Person

Arrange an opportunity for your children to interview someone that you consider to be wise and accomplished in life. This keeps them familiar with carrying on dialogue with adults and causes them to think on their feet in a conversational manner. Help them write out a list of questions that are pertinent to that person's background. Here are some questions to get you started:

- What advice do you wish you would have received at my age?
- What were your most profitable investments? (Could include money, or investments of time, relationship and skills.)
- What are your favorite memories from the best times of your life?
- What do you consider as being most important to you at this time in your life?
- Which books, newspapers, magazines and other information sources do you study?
- What has been the greatest influence in your life?
- Who are your mentors? What can you tell me about them?
- If you had it all to do over, what is one thing you would do differently?

*If there is anything we wish to change in the child,
we should first examine it and see whether it is not something
that could better be changed in ourselves.*
~ Carl Gustav Jung

*The best training any parent can give a child
is to train the child to train himself.*
~A.P. Gouthey

Goal Setting

Navigating the Course

Having navigated many bodies of water, I have come to respect the art of chart and map making. If I had been an explorer in the early centuries, I doubt any king or queen would have offered me an all-expense paid trip to chart the new world. The moxie of those explorers is something to marvel over: such big, audacious visions that they dared to believe in and set the necessary goals to accomplish. I admire that ambition to make one's dream a reality.

As a parent, I feel it is my responsibility to teach my children to map out the journey before them. If we purposefully show our children how to plan for an abundant life, they will have an advantage. A wise parent will ask the right questions and direct the steps of planning for education, career and marriage.

Through many engaging experiences, good books, and influential relationships we place before them, our children and grandchildren gain a broad view of just how abundant life can be for them. Teaching them to navigate this course toward attaining their life goals is like teaching a man to fish. It sets them up for life.

Give a man a fish and you feed him for a day.
Teach a man to fish and you feed him for a lifetime.
~ Chinese Proverb

Setting the Course

In the summer of 1965, my wife Velda and I set out for our first boat trip through the San Juan Islands with our three older children all under the age of ten. Imagine this: We were on a 21-foot boat with a small cabin and a 35-horsepower, manual-start engine. We were a family set for a weekend of great fun and adventure. Equipped with a navigational chart in one hand and a highway map in the other, I was "ready."

Let me first tell you what I didn't know. I didn't know much about tides and charts, I didn't know about currents, and I didn't know about magnetic north. I did have a Navy surplus compass sitting on the floor of the boat between my feet. This is all true, and right now the avid boaters who are reading this are curling up the corners of the page with sweaty palms, and thinking some pretty incriminating thoughts about this novice on the water.

The plan was to spend the first night in a slough; the only problem was there were no docks. No problem. I had to continue showing my family that everything was under control, so I tied up to a piling for the evening where we had dinner in very cramped quarters and played games. I went to nearly desperate lengths to show my family what fun boating was going to be for us.

The next morning we set out to continue our journey. Like any explorer would, I wrapped my bearing around the confidence of a few fixed points, consulted my charts, propped my feet up on the Navy compass, still packed in the box, and headed out for the day into what I now know are not navigable waters. By 10:00 am we were stuck on a thick, stinky, gritty mudflat where we stayed until the tide came back in around 3:00 that afternoon.

My popularity with my family tanked, but my enthusiasm was not washed out. In my estimation, this was an exploration with only a few small glitches so far. To salvage a bit of this story, and a morsel of my pride, I will let you know that we did finally arrive at Jones Island where we camped and had a wonderful time.

I'll spare you some of the details of this voyage where I felt akin to great explorers like Columbus, whom you will remember set out for one destination and ended up in another. As we left Jones Island, a dense fog settled in and my field of vision was extremely limited. Although I left it sitting on the floor, I did at least consult the trusty compass—yet to be removed from its packing box.

We cruised for hours through heavy fog without seeing any sign of land, and for quite some time I had absolutely no idea where we were. With my daughter crying, and my wife being both scared and furious with me for my lack of preparation, I began commiserating in my mind with Henry Hudson, who faced mutiny by his own crew while trying to find the Northwest Passage. Matters were coming to a head, and my saving grace was a man dressed in Navy dungarees standing on the seashore in the lifting fog.

"How did you get here?" he hollered. "I knew you were in trouble and decided I better come down to the beach to help, because we *never* get boats in this part of the island."

This generous Navy sailor waded into the water, fully clothed, to keep our boat off the rocks. Meanwhile, a different Navy man came to our aide, and to assist them, I used an oar to push us off the rocks. In the struggle, the ore broke and I lost the setting from my ring. One more mishap from this day.

Just to test my memory on this, I recently took a few moments to consult a navigational chart of the area of this voyage. I can see where we started and many of the places we went. However, the location where we ended that day is so far off of this chart, it appears half way across my desk, and very near to my water glass. Someday I may take the time to figure out the exact number of miles that we were pushed off course by currents and wind, but for now, let me just say, it was *way too far*. It's a wonder we ever became a boating family!

Raising a family is a lot like taking a voyage; success is dependent upon a clear plan with an exact destination, good communication, and the right equipment for a successful voyage. Now that I am more experienced, I would not take my boat out on the water without first educating myself. I needed to have an understanding of all aspects of proper operation, and an exact route laid out to get to the chosen destination. There are dangers in the water just like there are dangers and obstacles in life. It will pay off well to do a good amount of pre-planning for this journey. Always set a clear course to protect your crew and ensure a rewarding journey with an exact destination in mind.

The Big Question

Here is a question that I hope you will not answer too quickly, but will ponder until you get to the answer that expresses your deepest conviction.

What is your vision for your family?

Do not limit yourself. Dream a little here. Start by developing a clear picture of future success for your family and write down the specific goals to make it happen. Take a look at your family's current goals, assuming they have already been identified and written. Evaluate whether they are still relevant, or do you need a new vision for this new season in life?

Every family in this process will benefit from taking the time to write down their vision and the specific steps that will move them forward. From the youngest to the oldest, everyone should be involved in the execution of the plan.

One example of how to incorporate vision is, rather than rewarding your children with a vacation that just magically spins out of thin air, teach them about setting goals by bringing them into the planning process for a valuable learning experience.

- Ask each person to give their input on the goal. (A family vacation in this case.)
- Take everyone's ideas and send them off with research tasks to find interesting information about the locations they suggested for the vacation. Make sure they are learning through their involvement, and you are not doing everything for them.
- Have a meeting to discuss the options and narrow down the location. A parent may need to exercise his/her executive decision making authority based on what is reasonable for your family's situation, time and finances.

Small Goals Lead to Fulfilling the Greater Vision

We wanted our children to grow up with the perspective that they could reach their heart's desires if they just took the right steps. Life is full of rich opportunities, and setting worthy goals as individuals and as families will keep life healthy, vibrant and growth-oriented. Without a vision, action plans, and structure, families will tend to be blown off course and exist without a worthy direction.

One man had a vision for his family of ten children to all play musical instruments together and eventually use this talent to bring joy and encouragement to others. He spent many hours praying over his vision and felt that the plan was quite clear. He set small goals, which included different mentors, music lessons, exposure to talented musicians, and eventually, recording their own album. Each goal was a step closer to realizing the ultimate vision of a family who traveled together putting on musical performances and selling their CDs.

As the family strategist, you may be the person who sets the example of vision casting and goal setting. Doing this will instill good habits for your children to carry on in their own families. As you lead in the example of family and personal goal setting, the kids will become more engaged and feel they have an actual purpose in the greater plan.

Family Meetings

Sunday evening was family meeting night when our kids were young. Steaming mugs of hot chocolate and a plate of snacks were the main draw to get them gathered around the table. There we would initiate a discussion about the things we wanted to accomplish. We always asked for the children's input so they would get excited and feel ownership in this goal as well. Here is one of the ideas we tossed around the family meeting table:

"What do you think of hosting a foreign exchange student?" I asked.

"Where from?"

"How long?"

"Where would he or she sleep?"

Quickly, everyone was pouring in their thoughts and plans to make this the most exciting stay an exchange student could have experienced.

"We could take them boating, and to Seattle to visit the Space Needle."

As a family, we set about making detailed plans for this student, and since our student was coming from Germany, we also had our children do some research on Germany, so they would be well-informed hosts.

Other times the goals would be rather simple and short-term, like mentioning a need of a neighbor or family member who was ill, and asking the kids to figure out how we could be of help.

When the vision was for something with larger stakes, like attending college or taking a family vacation, the detail of the plans became necessarily more specific.

Regardless of the size of your ultimate goal, the steps you take to get there will succeed when they are well planned.

How to View Goal Setting

Let go of constraints and focus on how attaining this goal will change you and your family's life. Wrap your mind around the value of owning this one. It's alright if others see it as being overly ambitious. It is not about them. This is your goal, and you and your family are probably the only ones who need to be fully committed to the action steps.

Make the Goal Clear and Measurable

Write the small goals out on paper, and place them in a visible spot. Cross off each accomplished step. By breaking the larger goal into small steps, you are able to see progress and feel the satisfaction of knowing you are getting there. I check my lists of goals like a personal report card to make sure progress is happening as planned.

Test the Goal

Does this goal excite and motivate you and your family? Does it matter to you, or are you doing this for someone else? You must be personally motivated or you will lose sight of the purpose.

Is this goal measurable and life changing? Is it appropriate for this season in your life? Will it stretch you and even take you out of your personal comfort zone at times as you get closer to reaching this goal? Family commitment to the goal is essential; otherwise, the vision will slip away, because they won't take mental ownership of the process.

Commit to the Goal

Focus and commitment to the plan changes what "might be" into what "will be" for your family.

What is the first step you must take? Who will you need to help you? Bring in people who will help you and hold you accountable if needed.

Life is progressive, and without developing a big vision with specific steps to attain it, you will miss out on a multitude of experiences that could have been yours to enjoy.

Potential Obstacles

Have you ever been jerked back to reality when you discovered a plan you had set into motion was headed for failure? A bombardment of unforeseen obstacles is often the Achilles' heel of good intentions. Just like any good leader, you must identify all the possible obstacles to your goal in advance and know what you will do about them, if and when they occur. Anticipate discouragement and problems along the way, but do not let them derail your opportunity to attain a goal that is personally important to you or your family.

Many years ago one of my personal friends and mentors was Dr. Walter Burke. He was the CEO of McDonnell Douglas Aerospace Corporation and known as the "Father of the Space Age." Dr. Burke was wildly inspiring to me for many reasons, not the least of which was that he never stopped setting personal goals and living a large life.

Even though he was the CEO of an aerospace company, he didn't have his own pilot's license. He told me it was something he always wanted to do and was going to make certain he got one day. True to his word, Dr. Burke did all the work required to obtain his license to fly his own plane, a four-seat Cherokee Arrow. Yours truly has some great memories of circling the borders of the U.S. with him in his little plane.

When President Kennedy was in office, he called Dr. Burke, asking him to take up the audacious prospect of putting a man in space. The president said, "Now, Walter, you go ahead and solve the problems to get the job accomplished!" The president was telling him to get a hold of this vision, overcome the obstacles, and take the specific, measureable, and timely steps to get this over the finish line.

Dr. Burke once said, "I learned many years ago that one large problem is really a collection of many little problems. The way to tackle an impossible problem is to break it down and solve the several little problems one at a time."

That's how they do it in rocket science, so it must work for a missile as small as a family.

Anchor Points

It is important for the entire family to be on board and understand the value of goal setting. Explain that we all need to have the same end result pictured in our minds.

Play the Puzzling Goal Game
Here is an activity to demonstrate the importance of visualizing the end goal:

Purchase two identical puzzles. Divide your family into equal teams, or as close as possible. Give one team the puzzle with the box top showing the picture of the completed puzzle. The other team will only have the puzzle pieces and no picture. Watch as the team without the picture struggles to complete the task and see how much longer it takes to finish the puzzle.

Point out that we reach our goals faster when we have a clear picture of what it takes to get there. Writing out your goals is like seeing the picture before it is completed.

Engage in Meaningful Conversation with Family Members
- Where do you see yourself a year from now? Five years? Ten years?
- What are the specific steps you are taking now to assure the arrival of your goals?
- What is going really well in your life right now? To what do you credit that?
- Are there any changes that you would like to see take place in our family?
- What is your dream job?
- What kind of education would you like to have?
- Would you like to meet a friend of mine who could help you attain some of your goals?

- To whom do you look for information or advice? (Be specific: Who is this for you in our family, from sports, politics, etc?)
- What scares you?
- What is the best piece of advice you've received?
- What is your biggest regret? How can you make a comeback?
- What is the craziest thing you have ever thought of doing?
- If you could do anything for a living and be guaranteed of its success, what would that be?
- How do you want your grandchildren to think of you?
- Do you believe in luck?
- What do you think is the most important skill for a mom or dad to have?
- What do you think is a big waste of time?

Define Your Desires for Your Family
What do you want for your family, and how are you going to ensure that you will arrive at the goals and destinations that you have in mind? Start a list and write out the steps for attaining this goal.

Watch Your Response
When your children and grandchildren of all ages share their goals and ambitions with you, be sure to show your excitement for them and offer help if needed and wanted. Your positive energy will push them to continue their hard work. A positive and optimistic outlook will propel them toward their worthy goals. If they see doubt or fear in your eyes, they will likely lose confidence. Get behind those kids!

Discipline

Discipline is not just about finishing your homework on time.
It is also about leading a good life with principles.

My mother and father did not raise three well-behaved children without having to practice corrective discipline from time to time. If I was doing something that needed to stop immediately, my mother might give me a sharp rap on the posterior with a piece of kindling that was always nearby to start our wood stove. "Ouch," I would respond, but it was harmless and served well to get my attention.

Actually, I preferred this type of discipline because it was simple and quick. If my crime was more serious, she would make me sit in a chair for an hour, which was an agonizing amount of time for an active, restless boy. If the offense needed correction that got my attention even more, she would ramp it up a bit by canceling my allowance for a week or have me *"wait until my father got home."* Dad would deal with the offense with either a few memorable swats to my backside, or by having me walk with him through our greenhouses while he was working. The hardest part was waiting through long periods of silence, followed by a discussion of my deed and the inevitable consequence.

Becoming a dad revealed to me the truth that dispensing discipline truly is harder than submitting to it. There is always the risk of your children interpreting the discipline as a lack of love. In reality, discipline is a form of love that is more real than a kiss or hug, because a parent is putting his or her own popularity and image at risk to administer it.

Sadly, parents who do not discipline are setting their children up for a lot of unnecessary pain in this world. Unruly, untrained children will never know the amount of opportunities lost to them. Whether it is a four year old or a twenty-four year old, others will not care to contend with their uncivilized behavior. This comes at a great cost when they are denied the full benefit of relationships with quality friends and family, who simply pull away and avoid time with this child. Who could blame them?

If parents do not discipline their children, the world will. It will come later in life and it will be far harsher than the caring correction of loving parents. Discipline teaches respect; if we don't discipline our children, they will laugh at respect. They need to know and society needs for them to know that there are boundaries.

I have only respect for my parents and no resentment toward them for their efforts to help me grow up strong and wise. If more parents were like them, the world would be a safer and more pleasant place.

Life is a perpetual instruction in cause and effect.
~ Ralph Waldo Emerson

Learning from Natural Consequences

Discipline is about forming character in the child through cause-and-effect training. It is a series of activities that teach and form the child into a temperate member of society. If an adult leaves a valuable item laying around someplace, it is quite possible the item will be stolen or damaged by someone else, which serves as a natural bit of discipline for the adult. Hard lessons learned through dealing with naturally occurring consequences make us wiser in the long run.

Likewise, a child can learn much from the natural consequences for their actions. If a bicycle, scooter, or other favorite piece of play equipment is repeatedly left in the yard, driveway, or even down the street and unattended, the wise parent will take that item to the garage and place it up on hooks or a high shelf. Stepping up as a parent and saying, "This item is off limits for a week," is a lot easier than saying, "The Smiths backed over your bike when you left it lying in the driveway." Teaching respect of all property is very important.

One mother made use of what she called the Saturday Box. All the children knew the expectation was to pick up all personal items before going to bed each night. Any toys left out would be picked up by Mom and placed in the Saturday Box, which meant they did not get to have that prized toy until Saturday.

One day I looked over and saw my neighbor standing in his driveway. Hands on hips, and shoulders shrugged, my exasperated neighbor lamented over how sick and tired he was of his 16-year-old son's behavior. This young man showed no respect at all for family tools and equipment. With great disregard, he would leave things lying around with no plans of coming back to take care of them.

"I told Toby five times this week to roll up this hose and put away the bucket. He left it out here in the driveway after washing his car three days ago, and he just ignores me!"

I felt for my friend in his frustration, but when he went on to say that he was so frustrated he was just going to go "do it himself," I stopped him and offered a different approach.

"What would Toby learn from you just going and doing the task for him? Wouldn't that just reward and reinforce his negative behavior?"

At wit's end, my neighbor did not know what else to do. Every time he pulled into the driveway and saw the hose and bucket still there, he fumed over his son's cavalier disregard for family property.

I suggested that as soon as his son returned that afternoon he should walk him out to the driveway and walk him through the expected protocol. He would need to get on one end of the hose and have Toby grab hold of the other end. Step by step, as he showed his son how this was all to be done properly, he could also have a conversation about why it isn't good to leave these things out. This should all be done with the intent of keeping the relationship intact as a father coaching his son, without being condescending, and bringing his son up to a new level of responsibility.

Later, this neighbor told me he had taken my advice and even walked with his son into the garden shed and showed him where to hang up the hose. Remarkably, it was the same location where the boy had found it originally!

The younger generation learns nothing from the nanny system of walking around behind them taking care of everything they should have done themselves. Take the time to pattern their behavior by working side by side on the tasks needing to be done and the behaviors you expect to be practiced. When a frustrated parent just does the task for the child, nothing of value is learned. In this case, the discipline could have forged a new habit by a father working through the steps more relationally, and yet still holding his ground.

Keys to Effective Discipline

- Administer consistent discipline when your children are young; it is too late to gain that ground when they are grown.
- Correct in private and praise both publicly and privately.

Discipline

- Correction should occur without anger from the adult and should be soon after the offense.
- Think through your discipline. Will it be effective? Does it match the misbehavior? Will your child respect it when they look back as an adult?
- Never allow derogatory talk. This includes both speech toward the child or coming from the child. Words may carry some emotion, but must be respectful and well controlled.
- The child needs to feel restored and forgiven once the correction has taken place. Engage in a simple task or activity together and never use the silent treatment.
- Never deny eye contact during correction, as that can be interpreted as a lack of love. Get at the child's eye level to talk. Demonstrate that the relationship is still intact.
- Talk over the wrong-doing with the child and communicate what the behavioral expectations are for the future.
- Allow discipline to be a learning and mentoring time with the child. Seek teachable moments.
- Don't bring up the past. Once the discipline is over, it's over. The child should not be teased or reminded of the offense by any family members.
- Be consistent. If it is wrong today, it is wrong tomorrow as well.
- Do what you say you are going to do. Make no idle threats. If the parent says there will be a consequence for something, there must be follow through with the promised action.
- Make behavioral expectations clear.
- Don't allow back-talk, yelling, or slamming doors.

Effective discipline will take energy and focus from fully engaged parents. You can do this. Your children will feel more secure and loved when they know you care enough to enforce boundaries and good expectations.

Some People's Children!

I think every one of us has had the misfortune of entertaining the company of a child who has never received a morsel of correction. Let's just call it what it is, UNPLEASANT. These little urchins can turn your living room upside down in a matter of minutes, or climb over your shoulder on a tour bus where you thought you were on vacation. This might be a child who screams his head off in a nice restaurant while the parents, completely unaffected, just muse over how cute the child is. Even worse, some unaware parents just walk away, seeing no problem at all with the behavior. After all, we wouldn't want to squelch their personalities, would we? This form of parenting teaches the child to be a demanding, self-centered individual. Those traits do carry forward into life and can have devastating results.

Be encouraged when I say that children need and want boundaries. They are counting on their parents to provide the love and security that comes from well-defined boundaries and social courtesy training.

Metaphorically speaking, children will be ruled by the rudder or the rock. Being the rudder that guides a child with loving discipline will teach them good habits for a profitable life. Without a rudder to guide them, their boat may be torn to shreds on the dangerous and careless rocks of life. Children need parents who will be the rudder and dispense thoughtful discipline—and those parents need grandparents who are supportive and will back them up.

Postmodern Parenting

Now would be a good time to counter the culture that has formed around us with regard to discipline of children. Postmodern parenting has ventured away from obedience and parent-directed behavior, and is now in favor of allowing children to flourish through self-directed behavior choices and personal autonomy. The point of being a parent is to "train up a child in the way he should go." That is ancient biblical advice, and it is as relevant today as it was when it was written. Appropriate behavior must be shaped through the expectations put into place by parents who are willing to set standards, lay out boundaries, and even say "no," when necessary.

Parenting isn't about winning a popularity contest. At times you will feel exhausted. Giving full-time guidance can be tiresome. It is not overbearing; as a parent, it is your responsibility to love your children so much that you ask where they are going, when they will be home and whom they will be with. A loving parent may even show a bit of anger, disappointment or a few tears when the training process gets tough. Because of your love for them, you will be willing to train them by standing watch over a project which is taking them hours to complete and would have only taken you 15 minutes. You are the parent. You are training them, because you love them enough to take the time. As a parent, you will also love them enough to admit when you did something wrong and need to ask for forgiveness.

Teachable Moments

Catching "teachable moments" is essential to effective correction in behavior. Redirecting a child by bringing him alongside you with a "time-in" rather than a "time-out" will build self-esteem and train him in the way he should go. Time-out, or denial of a privilege, has its place as well, but requiring the child to cooperate and work on a project or chore alongside you can be a very healthy choice in training.

Example: One sibling sticks out his or her foot to trip another sibling who is walking by. The parent could send the offender to spend time alone in his room, or the parent could choose a "time-in" approach.

"Bobby, it appears your feet need something more productive to do. Put on your shoes and come outside to help me carry wood to the wood pile."

The child is with you, being trained, and doing something much more productive. Stacking wood is not high on the list of most children's favorite activities and will be a good deterrent from "tripping-the-sibling" type mischief in the future.

Some well-meaning parents have taken away the privilege of attending functions such as church youth group, Scout meetings, 4-H meetings, choir rehearsals and the like, feeling that it would make a strong impression on the child to have to miss these enjoyable functions. The counterproductive part of this is that it takes the child away from character-building activities. These influences usually include values-based teaching and work that will form the child into a better person. Unless the problem directly relates to one of these functions, denying participation in such groups could be unproductive.

Many parents are doing a splendid job of raising their children with good discipline, and I applaud their efforts. It is not easy these days. Setting standards with children when they are young will produce adults who are self-disciplined people with respect for authority and who are respectable people themselves.

Anchor Points

Teach Self Discipline

Respect and cooperation will rise when our children see us holding ourselves to a high standard. Demonstrating a life of self-discipline is challenging. We don't usually look at ourselves to see where we need to improve, and then work through the specific steps to make a change.

Books to read on parenting and discipline:

- *Parenting: The Early Years* – workbook and leaders' guide by Les and Leslie Parrott
- *Dare to Discipline* by James Dobson
- *Love and Logic* by Foster Cline and Jim Fay
- *Creative Correction* by Lisa Whelchel

Put Others First

This could be the only point we need to make, because it's at the root of all the others. This principle is manifest in holding doors, stepping aside, offering the last cookie, giving up your seat, changing a tire, carrying groceries, offering a hand. Putting others first means always saying, "Please, after you..."

Use Creative Correction

Here are some examples:

- Slamming doors
  When a child starts a habit of throwing a tantrum with the punctuating sound of a slamming door, Dad can remove the door from the hinges for a week.
- Teen who sneaks out at night
  Once the parent realizes this has occurred, get into that child's bed and be there when he or she returns!

- **Sour words spoken to another**
  If a certain child is having trouble curbing the problem of mean or sour talk to another family member, have that child take a hammer and a nail out to an old fence post and nail it in every time the offense needs to be addressed. After a few times, tell the child to go pull the nails out. Then ask him to describe what he sees. Each nail, representing harsh talk, is gone; the hole, or damage, still remains. Even though we try to remove the damage of our words with an apology, the damage was still done. Follow with a discussion about the scars some words leave on another person.

From Conflict to Forgiveness

The strength of a family, like the strength of an army,
is in its loyalty to each other.
~ Mario Puzo

Finishing Well

Failure is part of the deal in parenting. We don't always see what is coming at us or respond the way we ought. Embrace the lessons you learn through these times and know that today's failure is not the sum total of who you are as a parent.

In 2006, when my friend, Ted Engstrom, was nearing the end of his life, I asked him what advice he had for me. His reply: "Finishing well is more important than the journey!"

Ted had been the leader of many Christian organizations, including serving as President and CEO of both World Vision and Youth for Christ. His uncompromising commitment to serving the poor, coupled with a profound sense of business and managerial savvy, had a strong impact on the success of these ministries as well as on those of us who were close to him.

Those words, "Finishing well is more important than the journey," have rung in my ears with resounding hope for the

117

many excellent things that can happen in a person's life, even after a devastating setback or catastrophe within a family.

At some point in life, every one of us finds ourselves in the eye of the storm where things feel out of control and desperate. Instinct will bring out the fight in us, or we may turn to denial to avoid the trembling feeling beneath our feet. The wiser person is the one who allows the storm to refine and form their character.

Whether it is the loss of a dream, a loved one, or personal reputation, that conflict or event needs to be understood for the toll it took on you, your family and others, but it should not become a permanent barrier within a family. Everyone who honestly seeks forgiveness and restoration deserves the hope of a new tomorrow and time to move on, once again living with purpose and significance. Time must be taken to process the impact of the devastation, and part of that process is making the choice to finish well.

Playing the Parent Card

My daughter Kathy is a very perceptive businesswoman. She has an eye for what's right and what is not. She is not afraid to step up to the plate and let you know if something is going wrong. At one point, her husband was working in my company, and Kathy was feeling extreme pressure as she was squeezed between her husband and her husband's employer: me. What I didn't grasp was, while I was keeping my eye on the daily operations of the business, my astute daughter saw something much more massive growing. She was feeling the early tremors of a magnitude nine family and business quake, but I was not listening to her warnings.

Kathy recognized a deep crack in the inner workings of our business, but I was not ready to face it. I had experience, knowledge, and leverage on my side. I also had pride, fear and

118

denial working overtime, and I was not about to admit we had a problem. So, what did I do? I played the "parent card." It could not be trumped on the business level; therefore, everyone kept up business as usual, and, out of respect for me, didn't question my direction. The problem was that my lack of communication and receptiveness drew the personal conflict between my daughter and me to a peak. The reasons for that were also mounting up on the rest of the family. I suggested we see a counselor to help us work through the issues, and Kathy agreed.

Nothing makes a relationship stronger than when all parties are willing to come together to listen, learn, and communicate, all with the end goal of mutual forgiveness and restoration. The personal side of our conflict was able to be resolved because we were both willing to take steps toward forgiveness and healing. It is highly important in families that we do not put up walls and carry grudges. Collect rare coins or stamps, but don't collect grudges and bitterness; they have no redeemable value at all.

What We Perceive

What we perceive is not always reality. When we look at a stick in the water, it appears to be bent, but when we take the stick out, we discover the stick is straight: water distorts our perception of the stick. We must be very careful, therefore, when we argue that something is exactly as we have perceived it to be. This is particularly important when we make assumptions about the judgments, thoughts, motives and actions of other people. The truth is not always readily apparent to our senses, and therefore, we must not be quick to make judgments based simply on what we have observed with our five senses.

In relationships, we must be careful when arguing our own point of view, because things are not always exactly as we have perceived them to be. This is particularly true when making assumptions about the motives and actions of other family members. The truth is not always readily apparent. Take time to gather as much information as possible, and if you are going to make assumptions, assume the best.

A Forgiving Attitude

Sooner or later in any relationship, someone will be wronged. It is amazing how tolerant we can be of our own flops, but desire restitution from those who have crossed us. Forgiveness is tough, but the ones who benefit the most are those who "bury the hatchet," with a willingness to release and restore the offender.

What about the obnoxious buffoon who never says "I'm sorry," or never accepts responsibility in any way? In practical terms, we do need to keep boundaries with repeat offenders. But, as long as we are not talking about a dangerous person, those boundaries do not need to be as impenetrable as an armed fortress. Truly remorseful people need and deserve second chances and restoration within their family.

Parents and grandparents who set a family-wide example of living a forgiving attitude will set in motion an expectation that "in our family we resolve conflict in healthy ways." Nursing grudges and speaking poorly of family members will have a terrible ripple effect that only prolongs the pain. Unforgiveness yields oneself into the control of the other person. Forgiving another person will free you from the burden of anger and the desire to retaliate.

Starting at a young age, we attempted to teach our children to steer clear of tit-for-tat squabbles. Hopefully, by starting young, the habit will continue into adult life where the conflicts often have much larger stakes.

Healthy Ways to Work it Out

- Talk Face to Face
  Have you ever heard stories about the impressive conflict resolutions which take place when one person writes out his or her feelings and sends it to the other? Me neither! Too many misunderstandings happen from written messages. If at all possible, talk in person.

- Don't Offer Excuses
  Never ruin an apology with an excuse. Do not try to excuse or explain why you did something that was wrong, inconsiderate, or offensive. Just apologize for the impact it had on the other person. Express your sorrow and regret.

- Express Regret
  Use these words: "I'm sorry." "Will you please forgive me?" "I was wrong, can we work this out?" "I really regret my words/actions." "I owe you an apology."

- Take it on the Chin
  Accept the consequences of your actions or offer restitution, if possible. After all, you are being sincere; let your actions show it.

- Process
  Realize that complete healing and restoration is a process and will take time. Not time to build up walls and nurture ill feelings, but time to see change and work through emotions.

- Deal with Anger
  Talk with a trusted counselor, or write a letter to the person you have a grievance against and rip it up before mailing it. Process your feelings, but don't nurture the angry feelings. Deal with it, don't be trapped by it. Realize the harm resentment will have on your health and relationships.

- Pray
  Ask God to help you forgive. Say the Lord's Prayer and insert the offender's name: "Forgive me my trespasses as I forgive _____." If you are on the other side of the coin, pray about it. Choose the high road, face your wrongs, and ask to be forgiven.
- Learn from Others
  Read stories about people who have forgiven and restored relationships that were possibly more serious than your own. Take courage from the testimonies of others.
- Negotiate
  Be willing to allow room for give and take. Each party may need to make changes. Do not fight for anything that truly doesn't matter. Be willing to search for creative solutions.
- Assess
  Take an assessment of exactly what habits or patterns caused the conflict. Make a sincere study of the factors which created the situation and work to make sure the mistake or pattern does not recur.
- Affirm the Relationship
  Once the conflict is resolved, it will be necessary to follow up with a comfortable activity where things feel like they are back to normal. This is an essential step. Skip this step, and ill feelings will undoubtedly creep back in.

I'll Catch You When You Fall

Do you remember the 1992 Olympic athlete Derek Redmond? During his career, he held the British record for the 400 meters, and won numerous gold medals. Unfortunately, a series of injuries blighted his career, and now he may be best remembered for his performance at the games in Barcelona,

Spain, when he tore his hamstring in the 400-meter semi-final. Pressing on, he fought through the pain, and with the assistance of his father, managed to complete a full lap of the track as the crowd rose to a standing ovation. TV highlights of the incident illustrate the Olympic spirit and great courage.

The image of Derek's family cheering him on from the stands is the iconic picture of family support. His father, running onto the track and putting his arm around his son's waist to give him support to finish the race, sums up the mission and spirit of an interdependent family. These families share the same goals and values, with a willingness to work cooperatively to make it over the finish line.

There is no greater joy and satisfaction than seeing your family working together and supporting each other. Through times of high achievement, as well as turbulent trials, everyone desires to know their family will be there for them.

Several members of our family have come through particularly difficult times of their own, and each would attest to their faith in God and the support of family that got them through. When families have established these healthy relationships, it is a natural outpouring to support each other through times of turmoil. The key is to establish the healthy, relationship-building patterns of a loyal family before the time of trial hits.

Onward!

Life is not without its setbacks and disappointments. Will you let those setbacks stop you? Cripple you? We will make mistakes, and at times, will have strife with the people we love the most. Any of us in a family may act in ways that bring embarrassment upon the family, and there may be times when you wonder if the infrastructure of your family can handle the strain without breaking. The question is: Will we hold these events against each other and be mortified by them, or will we allow them to strengthen us and be modified by them? Strength comes when we allow ourselves to be changed for the better by the events around us. In the long run, we become a more loyal family with a tenacious spirit for pressing on.

I have lived through seven generations of a family that has held together through thick and thin, which has set a positive precedent for all the generations. We do not give up on each other, and we do not give up on ourselves. Maybe that sounds like pressure, but I would call it positive pressure. In those seven generations, there has yet to be a single divorce. This is unheard of in this age of moving on when things get too tough or inconvenient.

The keys are to stay the course, remember your moral compass and find your way back to the joy of those simple things. The trials faced today will not last forever, but family will, and the extraordinary blessings of everyday, ordinary life will sustain you.

If you or your family has been through the crippling effects of some personal disaster, I have one strong word for you: *Onward!* This is no time for stopping. Keep on keeping on. Onward!

If you cannot get rid of the family skeleton,
you may as well bring it out and make it dance.
~ George Bernard Shaw

Anchor Points

Understand the Word "Commitment"
A commitment is a pledge or promise that you intend to keep. Great relationships work through storms and gain strength through long-term faithfulness.

Connect with a Support Group
Individuals and families can benefit from the accountability of a support group and the accumulated knowledge and experience that is available there.

Seek Counseling
Be willing to seek professional help. This is not a sign of weakness. These professionals have ideas you have probably never considered and will help you live at peace, with a plan for reconciliation.

Take Responsibility
Resist the urge to place blame on others and always accept your part in whatever the turmoil is. There will be much less resistance for the person who humbly accepts their part in a conflict.

Ask for Forgiveness
Take deliberate steps to seek forgiveness and admit your mistakes. Speak with each affected person without offering excuses. With contrite spirit, the person who can say "I'm sorry" is a person of strength.

Finish Well

Always aim to better your best. Regardless of your track record up to this point, keep loving your family with more creativity, energy and adventure. Let your actions and words sincerely communicate how much they mean to you.

Love Gets Busy

Love is not something you feel; it is something you do.
~ David Wilkerson

I remember the day my father came to me and told me that the reality of his dad having passed away was really sinking in. I could tell this was particularly difficult for my dad since he and his father had been very close. We were standing in one of Dad's greenhouses when he put his arm around me and said, "You know, I always knew I could go to Dad if I needed 50 bucks."

It wasn't the promise of cash in hand that my father valued; it was that he knew his dad would be there for him if the chips were down. Dad was cut from the same cloth. I always knew I was welcome to borrow anything my father had. If he owned it, I could borrow it. My friend's parents would not even let them touch their tools. My best friend would come to our house to borrow our tools because his dad had theirs under lock and key.

Many times in life I have had a strong realization that, for love to be fully conveyed, it demands action. Love is never stationary; when it sees a need, it chases it down and does something about it.

Too often people want to put up walls. "It's too dangerous to love." "Love hurts." "I'll never love again." For some, love is like an island. They can see it and know it is there, but they never dive in deep enough to cross over to it. If people just allow themselves to love lavishly, the world would change overnight.

My dad showed me this type of love when he spent evenings lying on the concrete floor of our garage helping me as a teenager install a transmission in my old Ford. Dad viewed auto mechanics as something you only did if there was no other option. Even so, many times he would lie on a cold garage floor to help me work on my car, when I knew he would rather have been sitting in front of a fireplace with a good book.

Now, I watch my own adult children putting their desires and plans aside to put the needs and wants of their own children and grandchildren first. They willingly give up their weekend to babysit their grandchildren, because they understand the importance of their grown children having quality time alone for their marriage.

Love is an activity that we do. Much like a sport, you had better be suited up for the game, because you never know when you will be called off the bench to make a power play. Love is not a spectator sport like so many seem to view it. Oh, I don't think parents or grandparents are doing this on purpose, but just assess yourself to see if you are one who enjoys watching the younger generation from the sidelines or if you are in the game, stirring things up just to keep life exciting.

In his book *Love Does*, author Bob Goff writes: "Love is never stationary. In the end, love doesn't just keep thinking about it or keep planning for it. Simply put: Love does."

Living from the center of your heart doesn't have to be complicated. Love just gets up in the morning and gets busy, serving those you care about.

Understanding

Any fool can know. The point is to understand.
~ Albert Einstein

I know people whom I would describe as being wholehearted individuals. These are people who look past insignificant blemishes in another person and head straight to the heart. It's like they have an unstoppable superpower that sees right past the ugly and straight into the potential of an individual. They eagerly hold out their arms to embrace others, even when they are suffering themselves. They are interested in others and always want to understand them. They win people over, not because of what they offer, but because of what they bring out of others. Our children need this element in our relationships with them. They have a need to feel understood and heard.

Honestly, do you think you actually can relate to your children and grandchildren? Think of how things have changed over the last decade with regard to technology, employment availability and company loyalty, social media, and traditional roles in marriage and in the workplace. Nothing is the same. Am I suggesting feigning an attitude of understanding? No. This is where you get interested and seek to gain deep understanding.

What I do understand is what it feels like to forget a homework assignment and have to own up to it in front of a teacher. I understand how much your palms sweat when you want to ask a pretty girl out for a Coke. I understand the stress a young family feels when the paycheck doesn't stretch far enough to cover the mortgage, and a baby is on the way. And I understand the feeling of helplessness when a loved one is in critical condition. These are areas of understanding that do not change between generations.

There are times when our family members don't need to hear all that we know. They need to know that we understand and support them. Often, love puts its own opinions and ideas aside. This is when we spend more time listening, and only asking enough questions to pull out more of what the other person is feeling. The personal mission I try to live by with my family is this: *Watch, listen, cheer them on, pray for them and give advice only when asked.* The last one is the one I find the hardest to carry out, but I'm working on it.

Soren Kierkegaard once said, "Life can only be understood backwards; but it must be lived forwards." This perspective puts us parents, and especially grandparents, at a distinct advantage. We do have perspective on many topics, and that insight can help us build stronger intimacy in our relationships through listening and understanding. No lecturing or interrupting. Just give the gift of wholehearted acceptance and selfless love through understanding.

Building Understanding

Be aware of your body language, voice tone, and tendency to cut in and give unsolicited advice or to tell the other person why he or she should see things differently. Relationships grow and become more transparent as the basis of understanding grows.

Ask:

- "What are some of the things you are dealing with right now?" (Refer to a specific situation: school, work, relationship, faith, home repair, etc.)
- "What could be changed to make this situation better?"
- "What do you hope for?"
- "Is there anything I can do to be of help to you?"

The Greatest Threat

*People who really want to make a difference
in their family do it because of love.*

During an exclusive interview with former president George W. Bush, a reporter asked him what he saw as the greatest threat to the United States. Certainly this reporter was stunned when the answer had nothing to do with foreign adversaries. Instead, the president responded with concern that the greatest threat was the deterioration of the American family.

Our children are watching the interactions we have with our spouse. They are sharp students and are picking up strong signals, which will lead them either toward the success or the deterioration of their own families. Children are impressionable and vulnerable and will pick up behavior from their parents.

Research finds that children are more secure when their parent's marriage is the central relationship in the home. When they see mutual love and respect between their parents, they feel secure in their family and will remember this as the way to treat their own spouse one day.

It's the same with family conflict. When children see their parents working out every problem, they are learning the importance of keeping their promises and valuing relationships enough to work through problems. Simply stated and steeped in truth, the best gift you can give your children is to love your spouse.

My father often told my siblings and me how beautiful our mother was and how lucky we were to have her for our mother. I never heard my father put my mother down, and I never heard my mother put my father down. Oh, there were heated discussions, as there are in all marriages, but they never stormed off or ended with disrespect. On occasion, Mom would even shed a few tears over the conflict and Dad would kiss her to reassure her. If anything, this showed us how much they cared about the relationship, and hated those moments when it went awry.

I also remember the "D" word was never used or threatened in our home, and I would never have it in mine either. People who think life will get better after a divorce are caught up in a sordid myth. In most cases, a divorce only exchanges one set of problems for a different set of problems. Seeking counseling and changing habits to correct the painful course is often a far better choice. Both partners must be committed to this process.

Some of the truest and most valuable impressions parents can make on their children are how they treat each other, and the values they live out.

I still like the old-fashioned idea of families holding together and making it through the tough times. There will be tough times in every marriage. Ask any couple who stayed together and worked it out, if they are glad they did. Most will let you know it was the right decision, and life is good.

The message I want to send to my kids and grandkids about marriage is this: Marriage is not just about making the right decision. It's about making the best decision you can make, and spending the rest of your life making it right.

Sister Love

Don became my second son when I married his mother, Esther. Although Don is a bachelor, he has three sisters and a mother who keep him in pretty close check.

A while back, Don was experiencing some serious health issues for which the medical establishment seemed to have no answers. Symptoms could not be ignored, but doctors offered few solutions. A frightening time for anyone, but even more so when you live alone and have no one there for support and to act as your advocate. Well, this committed bachelor was not going stag to this event! His sister, Patty, was the first to make that clear by coming to his side.

Stepping up, Patty made numerous calls to doctors and got her brother admitted for extensive testing and care. Now, this bachelor with no woman looking after him, had four women looking after him, and the doctors knew they were serious about getting to the bottom of their concerns.

This is what love does. It brings out the advocate; it triumphs when there is a need; it is tenacious to the end. Love doesn't recognize inconvenience. When this brother and son had a need, love is what propelled the actions of his sisters and mother on his behalf.

Where the Rubber Leaves the Road

"Mr. and Mrs. Harmon, Wendy would like to speak with you in the living room."

It was quite late, and I didn't recognize this teenager who had just knocked on our bedroom door. My wife and I, who were ready for bed, looked at each other with bewilderment and figured we had better go find out what was up.

Earlier in the evening our youngest daughter, Wendy, had asked permission to take five friends with her in our car to the high school football game, so we had the feeling the evening may not have ended too well.

In our living room, a cadre of *twelve* teens greeted us, and all were well-prepared to give a ready defense of our daughter's innocence. Each one declared that even though Wendy was adjusting the radio at the time, the fact that she careened off the highway, through a field, and into a barbed wire fence was not at all her fault!

Life is messy. We all make messes. Some are rather small and others are colossal. Regardless of the size of mess any person makes, it is vital for the person to be forgiven and restored. Clearly, Wendy was concerned over how her mother and I would respond; hence the reinforcement of teenaged character witnesses.

Whether it is the young person who crumbles to temptation and steals a candy bar, the teenager caught in a pack of lies, or the adult who embezzled from the employer, when people make monumental mistakes and seek to be forgiven, they should be met with monumental love that forgives and restores.

Relentless love restores and forgives. This love is where the rubber meets the road, and working through life's messes together is where love is perfected.

Anchor Points

Think "That's Right!"
How are you expressing heartfelt love and commitment to your family? Take a moment to think of what you are doing right! Make a list and continue doing these things. I'll bet you are doing a lot that is right on!

Hold a Family Appreciation Dinner
Schedule a certain night on the calendar as family appreciation night. Each time this date comes around, announce which person from the family will be appreciated. Make sure everyone knows that, right after a special dinner, everyone will have the chance to talk about what they value in that person. Time between dinners may vary depending on the size of your family.

Memorize the "Love Verse"
With your family, memorize the following verse. Hang it in a picture frame or write it on your walls. Make it your purpose as a family to understand and live by these words:

Love is patient, love is kind. It does not envy, it does not boast, it is not proud. It does not dishonor others, it is not self-seeking, it is not easily angered, it keeps no record of wrongs. Love does not delight in evil but rejoices with the truth. It always protects, always trusts, always hopes, always perseveres.

Do the Little things that Say, "I Love You."
- Go through the entire day without complaining.
- Ask "What can I help you with today?"
- Do an activity together.

- Turn off your cell phone, TV and computer for an entire evening.
- Say "I really appreciate it when you _____."
- Pray for your family.
- Ask "What are some things we should try to do as a family?" Make plans to accomplish a few.
- Ask "What is your favorite memory of our family?"
- Watch family movies together or look through old pictures.
- Play a game together.
- Get everyone involved in making dinner.
- Take some silly family photos.
- Post pictures of family members in prominent spots around your work area. They will know you care when they see their picture there.

Movies:
- *Courageous*, Sherwood Pictures (2011)
- *Fireproof*, Sherwood Pictures (2008)
- *The Vow*, Screen Gems (2012)

Books:
- *Love Does* by Bob Goff
- *The Love Dare* by Stephen Kendrick, Alex Kendrick
- *The Five Love Languages* by Gary Chapman
- *The Bible*

Love doesn't make the world go round;
love is what makes the ride worthwhile.
~ Elizabeth Browning

Holidays and Celebrations

The best and most beautiful things in the world
cannot be seen or even touched. They must be felt with the heart.
~ Helen Keller

Have you ever wished you could permanently capture a moment in time like an indelible snapshot in your mind? Whether we are decking the halls for Christmas or stuffing plastic Easter eggs for the big hunt, I find myself reminiscing about past celebrations almost as if I'm flipping through my personal album of memories.

We will often start holiday parties early in the afternoon to give everyone a chance to include stopping by into their schedules. By twilight, it seems half the population of town has arrived at the doorstep, but usually it is just our immediate family of four generations. I should point out it is not the number of people that matter, because many times we have just gotten together with a small group. It is all about the opportunity to connect and build relationships with one another.

My wife, Esther, has a particular knack for entertaining. She will strategically fill a table in one room with a bountiful spread of confections while another room will have platters of savory fare. A beverage table will be laden with drink choices and crystal glasses lined up like chorus girls, and the voice of one of the great singers like Nat King Cole will waft through the background. Her hospitality is quite strategic, as it keeps people milling through the different rooms of the house and bumping into new folks, creating the opportunity to stop and chat. These warm scenes always fill my heart with the deepest sense of gratitude for the many blessings we have as a family.

Forego the Curmudgeonly Outlook

Holidays can be unnecessarily difficult as families with married children attempt to coordinate plans and gatherings that don't encroach on the plans and desires of others. It can be a time when emotions are at their peak and it is easy to step on toes. If we can just put all selfish desires aside for the moment and focus on the real goal of holidays, I think there is a possibility of finding some harmonious middle ground.

We always have an open door on holidays, and everyone knows they are welcome. There will be food and merriment whether it is just a few of us, or if the whole gang lands at the front door.

Time together is good and always warms the heart, but my wife and I try to make a point of alleviating any feelings of guilt if someone is not able to attend. We understand they have other family members to spend time with and, believe me, we want for them to have good relationships all the way around their families.

When someone in a family makes a mandatory tradition of everyone being in a certain place at a certain time, they are, in effect, making a tradition into a trauma. This wrings the genuine feelings of unconditional love and celebration right out of the event. If you have ever been a party to such mandates, you know how quickly they can become caustic.

Forego the curmudgeonly outlook on holiday and family celebrations. Give everyone your blessing to be where they need to be, and chances are they will be in your house, where they feel loved, accepted, and free.

All Inclusive

Hitting a grand slam within the family means getting all the players off the benches and into the game. Everyone must feel needed and wanted. When my wife was nearing a significant birthday, I called upon the "key strategists" in the family. I asked them to get the word out to everyone so we would have the best turnout possible. In the family email below you will see how one daughter formed teams and made everyone feel like an important part of the big picture.

Hello Family –
Dad/Phil, in his delegatory manner, has assigned Kathy and me to figuring out the menu for Mom's 75th Birthday Bash. You may already know that the party is March 9th. We as a family are going to provide the food, Phil will provide a ham and turkey. Kathy and I have assigned food/drink categories to specific family groups. It is up to those groups to get together and wow us all with their offerings. We are looking at feeding around 55 people – some quite small, but still.....

> *Kathy and daughters – Heating up the meats, potatoes for all and rolls/breads for all.*
> *Wendy and daughters – Veggies for all and salad for 20.*
> *Jewel and daughters – Salads for 40.*
> *Sandy, Bill, and kids – all drinks.*
> *Cheryl, Patti and Phyllis and kids – Mom's favorite desserts. . .*

So Gentlemen and Gentlewomen, start your engines, power up those emails and begin coordinating/cooperating with your teammates. If you have any questions, you can send them to Kathy or me.
Thanks, Cheryl

Cheryl's letter is effective because she has a whimsical tone that makes this sound like something fun and not to miss. While we don't want to pressure anyone into attending family gatherings, we do our best to give ourselves a reputation of inserting so much fun and surprise that everyone wants to be there.

Now what about the new family member or the socially shy person who feels uncomfortable? Think about who is coming, what they enjoy, and what puts them at ease. Let's say a granddaughter brings a new fiancé to a first family gathering. In advance of the gathering, I might call upon one of the guys in the family and ask him to make a point of chatting with this new individual. To keep things moving and comfortable, I would possibly suggest a couple of the men head out to the garage to look at my old collectable car, or get a game of flag football started up. Another idea is to give the new or shy person a task. Allowing them to have a purpose at the gathering is quite effective when trying to put someone at ease and make them feel a part of the big picture.

Thinking through the hospitality plans, and considering the personalities and preferences of the group are the keys to inclusive relationship building at family gatherings.

Set up some lively, interactive games for everyone to participate in, but be willing to let them go if the atmosphere shows they are just not necessary. Ideas:

- Indoor and outdoor games
- Game of family trivia (someone in the family can make this up)
- Ping Pong table in the garage
- Basketball hoop
- Fun food that requires active participation. Fondue, dipping caramel apples, pulling taffy, pressing cider, building your own shish kabobs, etc.

- Several conversation or game areas (Living room, dining room, etc.)
- Craft table
- No TV unless it is the point of the gathering, such as watching the Super Bowl.

By the way, this all-inclusive mindset for family gatherings is paying off in spades. As parents, grandparents and now great-grandparents, we revel in the opportunity to spend time with our family. The greatest compliment our kids and grandkids ever pay us is simply to show up when we have family gatherings or to call when they are in the neighborhood and say, "Hey, mind if we swing by?" or, "Are you available for dinner?" We love catching those moments with them.

Anchor Points

Here are some activities we have done over the years and ideas you may want to try with your family:

New Year's Eve
Invite family friends in for an evening of games and food, including plenty of noise makers!

Bag or Box of the Hour
Count down to midnight, starting earlier in the evening. Set out a large bag or envelope and write the hour on it. Inside each bag place a note announcing the activity for that hour and some of the necessary items to accomplish it. Examples:

7:00 pm – Game Hour: Place a well-loved and interactive game in the bag. (Charades, Pictionary, Mafia or Psychiatrist)

8:00 pm – Fondue Hour: Place a pot and skewers in the bag and have all the ingredients readily available to pull out of the refrigerator.

9:00 pm – Talent Show: Divide into teams and give everyone about 20 minutes to come up with their talent. The goofier the performances the better, though some will actually perform with amazing talent. Put on a show for everyone during the last half hour.

10:00 pm – Sharing Time: Depending on your group, you could show some photos of the past year or offer a time for individuals to share something they are thankful for from the year.

11:00 pm – Dessert Hour: Place the ingredients for a dessert in the bag. One idea is to have an ice cream sundae bar and put some of the toppings and an ice cream scoop in the bag.

12:00 Midnight: Fill this bag with party supplies, noise makers and sparkling cider.

The ideas for activities during each hour are limitless. Just think of what your particular crowd would enjoy.

Valentine's Day

Not just for lovers. Give small gifts, cards and notes to let your family know how much you love them. Make it into a family affair with a special dinner. Younger children and singles are especially happy to have something to celebrate on this day.

Easter

We invite our family to attend church, followed by brunch and an Easter egg hunt at our house.

Here is how we run the egg hunt: We divide the hunt into age appropriate categories and prizes. We first release the easier-to-find eggs in the front lawn for the youngest children, and then move to different areas and make them harder to find for the older ones. With the goal always to build memories and relationships, here is what we put inside our eggs:

- Coupon to have lunch with Grandma or Grandpa
- Money
- Candy
- Ticket to take to Grandma for a larger prize. (Kite, bubbles, coloring books, etc.)
- An invitation to go with Grandma to wave American flags in support of the military.
- Puzzle pieces. They have to get together with others who found puzzle pieces in the same color of eggs and be the first team to assemble the puzzle. The winning team gets a prize. The prize can be something nominal like a badge

they get to wear for the day that says, "I'm a winner!" Or it could be a tasty treat just for the winning team. Any prize will do, because this is all about the fun of doing the activity together.

Memorial Day

This is an ideal day for a family camp out or barbecue. When I was a boy my grandmother would take me to the cemeteries to decorate the graves. This is a good opportunity to teach about our military, as well as family history and roots.

July 4th

Get the gang together for a family potluck. Decorating our boat with flags, balloons, and banners for a patriotic cruise was one of our favorite activities for this day. Another idea is to have all the youngsters decorate their bikes for a bicycle parade. It only takes a couple youngsters to make up a family parade.

Thanksgiving

Growing up, I loved Thanksgiving for the opportunity to see aunts and uncles. Debates over cars, politics and theology always filled the air. I loved it!

Since our married children need to share this holiday with in-laws, we have started a tradition of getting everyone together for a game of flag football on the day after Thanksgiving. This builds up an appetite for some leftovers and time to reconnect.

Christmas

Since we now have married adult children, we have our main gathering at a time near Christmas to accommodate as many schedules as possible. This way everyone is free to be with their in-laws or immediate families on Christmas Day. If the day after

Christmas or a week before works better for everyone, we would move to one of those dates just as happily. This is one of those holidays that can cause strife if there is a mandate handed down to always be in a certain place.

During the Holiday Season

- Take one or two children along to deliver poinsettias to people who have been personal mentors, good customers, or teachers.
- Visit those who are elderly and shut in.
- Set a date for a one-on-one Special Day with each child. Usually, we would go out to lunch and get Santa pictures taken.
- Go Christmas caroling, or invite a bunch of folks in for some caroling around the fireplace.
- Decorate the outside of the house. When our kids were young our whole neighborhood got into the spirit of decorating. The creativity went to such a height we attracted bumper-to-bumper cars parading by the front of the houses. Wendy even dressed like an elf and I dressed as Santa, passing out candy canes and waving at the passing cars. It was our Christmas gift to the community. We loved it!

Christmas Gifts

All families have their own way of handling the exchange of gifts. Drawing names, or playing one of the gift exchange games, can all be very workable ideas. With the goal of relationship building in mind, here are a few ideas:

Secret Santa

Place everyone's name in a bowl. Let each person who is old enough to participate draw out one name. Taking part in a family Secret Santa can build excitement and anticipation during the season as everyone wonders who on earth is sneaking in to carry out these little surprises. The anonymous giver could have someone else deliver a cup of coffee, leave a note of encouragement, lift the burden of a certain task, hide a favorite piece of candy where only the intended person would find it, or have lunch delivered to their office. No one is expecting the Hope Diamond; small gestures are appreciated. Just make sure everyone who draws a name is onboard with the idea and will follow through. It never feels good to be forgotten by your Secret Santa.

Stockings

Ask each person to write notes of appreciation to slip inside the stockings of other family members.

Gifts of Time

Instead of purchasing store-bought gifts, consider giving the gift of time. Have each person or family come up with some sort of memorable outing or service to give as a gift. Here are some we have enjoyed exchanging:

- Weekend at the Cabin – One family, who owns a cabin, gave the gift of spending a weekend in this rugged retreat with all the food provided.
- Moped Day Trip – I offered a day trip on the mopeds with my wife and me. It was a day meant to be tailored around the interests of the recipient and would include lunch and sightseeing.
- Cookie of the Month – The gift giver delivered a platter of fresh baked cookies to the recipient once each month for a full year.

- Dinner for Six – My wife and I served as the cook and waiter for two of our adult children and four additional people for an evening of fine dining at our house.
- BBQ for Eight & Dessert Cruise – Our son and his wife, who live on a lake, offered an evening BBQ with a dessert cruise. The recipient of this gift was able to invite seven others to come along.

Wrapped in festive Christmas paper, each gift included something to explain the event. The gift I gave was "A Day Just for You." I wrapped a toy motorcycle and boat with a list of possible events for a day tailor-made for the personal likes of the recipient. What fun my grandson Tyler and I had!

Birthdays

When invited, we try to attend every individual's birthday party. However, in a family the size of ours, we have gotten creative with how we make sure each one is celebrated. Smaller families will find it easier to host individual celebrations.

Combined Daughter Birthday Dinner

Shhh . . . Why they were invited is a secret. They don't even know who else is coming. Upon arrival they find out it is the combined Daughter Birthday Party! My wife sets a beautiful table with a small potted flower at each of their places, to take home as a little gift. We cook a nice meal and have a birthday cake. It may be months before or after the actual birthday of most, but the point is we have another reason for celebration.

BBQ for all the Guys

Same idea as the combined daughters' birthday celebration, only in this case the guys show up and gather around the grill.

Give Them Something to Talk About!

There is something that I have become keenly aware of: our children and grandchildren will come to an event because there is fun, and they will stay because they are loved.

Living a family life enmeshed in creative, fond, and spontaneous activities is the thrill of a lifetime and an invitation to be a part of a bigger picture. We find that our younger grandchildren revel in the idea of being a part of this big clan and all the crazy things we do. In our family, we create exciting pictures of the future by making sure there is always one thing they can expect: the *un*expected!

Planning: Good Medicine for Our Marriage

Esther and I have, many times, set out on a road trip that may take us six hours or more, but find that the hours breeze by as we spend most of our time talking and planning for the things we want to do with our family. Making plans keeps us young and grows our relationship. Adventure is good medicine!

The planning portion of the event or outing is often the most enjoyable part for my wife and me. We take great pleasure in brewing up new ideas together, and it is good for our marriage to have something so fun to focus on as a team.

Esther and I come together like a couple of strategists in a command center as we pull together the details for our family activities. Sometimes those details are top secret because we get such a kick out of seeing their reactions as we hurl some of our zanier ideas at our kids. Other times, we deliberately bring different family members into the planning and scheming so they can feel the excitement of being on the "inside." Plus, our kids just have a lot of creative ideas of their own. This planning process is like a massage to our relationship; it brings excitement and fullness to our marriage as we focus on infusing life with doing extraordinary things.

These traditions and special days hold a prized place in my heart and memories for

One grandson said, "I really appreciate the creativity in this family. I mean, take last night for example (family roars with laughter and comments over zany dress-up night and hay ride). Grandma and Grandpa really make you do things outside your comfort zone, but they are right there doing it with us. I mean, they cruise all over town on their mopeds like they are some kind of Harley Czars.

the time in life when they were just right. As the children grow up and the family adds new members, we make appropriate changes in our celebrations to incorporate the shifting needs associated with these new stages in life. Thus, we introduced Daughter Day, Bachelor Boy Day, Sisters Weekend, and Bachelorette Showers!

Daughters Day

Once our daughters were older, and our family was filling out with new members, I decided it would be a good idea to switch

150

from individual days to a group day and call it Daughters Day. This way, not only would I have the pleasure of spending quality, memory-making time with these gals; they would also be able to connect with one another in an arena where there just really is more fun in numbers.

Pick a date, include the element of surprise, good food, something new to learn or interesting to experience, and you have a fabulous day ahead.

One year I took them all into a department store stocked with masses of hats on display. From floppy-brimmed sunbonnets to fashionable felt fedoras, there was something to fit each one's personal flair. I handed them each the same amount of money and told them that they had ten minutes to buy a hat. Any money they didn't spend had to be given back to me. Point being, dump the money and have a good time. Ready, set, go! Off they dashed, looking a little shocked from the lack of advance notice and the time limit on their selections, but they each found a suitable hat which made for a glowing group picture before the day was over.

Give it Away

It was a beautiful summer day in Seattle, where my daughters and I were walking along the streets, enjoying the sea-salt breeze, dwarfed by the high-rise skyscrapers and taking in the flavor of life that is purely Seattle.

Soon we found ourselves standing by Seattle's historic pergola in Pioneer Square where I gathered the gals around to explain our next caper, one I hoped would stretch them as individuals and linger in their minds for quite some time.

"Here is the plan," I explained, reaching into my inside jacket pocket. "I am giving each one of you a hundred dollars. You will have exactly one hour to give this money away to whoever you feel needs it. We will all meet at the restaurant for lunch. I want to hear all about your experiences over lunch. Your time has now begun. GO!"

It could have been any amount of money in any town. We see needs in different ways through different eyes. Off they scattered, some of them going in different directions, while others realized they could give more money and make a bigger difference if they pooled their funds together. I headed back to the restaurant to await their stories, eager to learn how this activity impacted each of them.

No surprise that in a city like Seattle there was a surplus of needs, so their only complaint was that they wished I would have given them more time to scope out places with needs and to be able to connect with the people there. Like all big cities, Seattle is host to countless folks asking for money on every street corner. This exercise wasn't a race to give it away; it was about understanding need.

On one of the side streets between Pioneer Square and our restaurant was a small, almost unnoticeable, doorway that led to a women's shelter. The gals who had decided to pool their money found this spot and knew instantly, this was where they wanted to make their donation.

Happy to see cheerful and caring guests tapping on their entry door, the overseer offered the ladies a tour of the shelter. She took the time to explain the life predicament of most their residents and also told them about the rules for living there, which required the women to work and stay clean from drugs and alcohol.

Over lunch, these daughters described how deeply they felt for the needs they had witnessed that day as they looked into the lives of others who had such forlorn stories of hardship. Each one painted a compassionate story of the people they encountered and how this experience stretched them and affected them.

Not long after this Daughters Day, I heard from Patty. She told me she and her husband Grant had gone back to this shelter and used their own money to help with some needed improvements to the facility. Those are the moments that send a zinger right through my heart. Seeing your own children make the conscious choice to go out of their way to touch the lives of others in a truly meaningful way shows they are the quality of people you have always hoped they would become.

It's important to look outside of ourselves and see the needs of people around us. At whatever level we personally are blessed, there is always something each one of us can give back to this world. There is goodness in teaching children of all ages to give, and to give generously.

Surprise Guests

Whether it is for a Daughters Day, Adult Mystery Weekend, Grandkid Weekend, you name it; I like to invite a surprise guest who will spice things up. Often this will include an undisclosed destination, which adds another element of intrigue to our outing. Exposing my family to fascinating people and experiences will increase their perspective and scope of life. Our surprise guests have included authors, historians, doctors, motivational speakers, professional athletes, journalists, wine connoisseurs and more.

It isn't that I personally know all these intriguing people. Rather, I make phone calls and find ways to connect with interesting people whom I would like to be guests at our family gatherings. This will open up their world and make them more engaging and more effective in their own circles of influence.

I invited Emmet Watson, a long-time Seattle Post Intelligencer columnist, to attend one of our Daughters Days. He was quite captivating as he chatted with us on the topic of local history. What was even more surprising to me was Emmet, being intrigued by our family dynamic, wrote about our Daughters Day in his column. Needless to say, we were honored by his article, and that he felt our family tradition was a worthy story for the Seattle P.I.

Galloping Right Along

Another time, the ladies arrived at the restaurant where we had arranged to meet, and noticed there were three extra seats. "Who is joining us?" they wanted to know. Soon my wife, Esther, walked in with The Galloping Gourmet, Graham Kerr, and his lovely wife Treena. Graham was a front-runner in the TV chef cooking show arena, coming into the living rooms of American housewives each day with his signature entrance of jumping over the sofa on his studio set and running through the stage kitchen with unequivocal enthusiasm for his culinary tips and recipes of the day.

This dynamic duo sat at our table over lunch and engaged us with conversational bliss regarding styles of dining and hospitality. They shared about their love of family gatherings and even let us in on the grandchildren's nickname for him: Graham Cracker.

This lunch went beyond the delight of the day and actually grew into a lifelong friendship with the Kerrs and their children. Years later, our granddaughters attended the same missionary training post, and were a part of each other's weddings. You just never know how things will turn out if you just pick up the phone and ask.

Every family gathering has the potential to be enriching in some way. It does take effort, thinking ahead and making a purposeful plan, but the fun of it is exhilarating.

Boys Bachelor Day

Clear the calendar; the boys are headed to town! Our annual Boys Bachelor Day was an established event for the menfolk in the family. Every year I took my son Steve and our daughter's spouses out for a day to remember. This particular year, not only were we going on our annual Boys Day, we were also welcoming a new member of the family. Our daughter Phyllis was about to marry Dave, or as we called him, "LB," for *Lover Boy*. Hey, part of the deal was to have a back-slapping, male-bonding kind of day.

Husky fever is big among football fans in Seattle, so each year I would secure tickets for one of the University of Washington's big home games. Afterwards we always went someplace fun with good food for dinner and loads of laughter.

Communication is essential when setting up these family outings. To ensure everyone had cleared their calendars for this important day trip, I sent out the following reminder. Notice the casual and humorous bent, which is key when you want to bring folks together for a good time.

To: *Boys*
From: *"The Old Man"*
Save the Date: *October 6th*

*This is the day for our annual **Boys Bachelor Day**.*
After the football game, we will head out for dinner, and lots of laughs. (Mostly at LB's expense, as we welcome him aboard the family ship.)
If you have a problem making it, special needs, or ideas, let me know. I'm finalizing plans.
Looking forward to seeing all of you!
Dad

We had a rollicking day of real male bonding and, most importantly, our daughter's soon-to-be husband had no doubt he was a welcomed member of our family. We have other traditions for welcoming new family members, which usually include something like a ski trip or boating with the guys.

Rolling out the welcome mat to new members of the family doesn't have to be elaborate; just make it sincere and F-U-N.

- Plan a party or unique outing to welcome the person into the family.
- "Step" children are never referred to as such. They are our children and grandchildren; no categorizing.
- Allow individuals to feel comfortable being who they are. Some like to sit and talk, while others need to go get fresh air and get away from the action to clear their heads. Let that be. We all act differently in social settings.
- Make opportunities for one-on-one conversation, either in person or by phone, with every member of the family. Don't only convey messages through your biological family members. Talking directly with spouses will send a message of full acceptance and family ties.

Bachelorette Shower

I marvel at how women create beauty. It must be an exceptional design that God placed in them from the beginning of time. When the women in our family put their heads together to make something special, the men look upon it like a newly found landmass that is absolutely mind-blowing. Women can't just put out a bag of chips, some beanie weenies and an ice chest of beverages. No, their breads and cookies look like flowers in the peak of summer and their drinks appear more like love nectar from the Greek gods. How they do it I do not know, but I admire it, and can fully appreciate that they have a gift for making things special.

The ladies in our family have a spectacular tradition for celebrating new brides. They take a whole day to make a fuss over her, complete with special meals, stories and games to create a jovial mood and close family connections. The unique thing about this day is that no one brings a gift. Instead, everyone sends in whatever amount of money they would normally spend on the shower gift. The money is all lumped together to purchase gift certificates. If there is any leftover cash, it goes into a cookie jar which the bride can dip into if needed in one of the stores. This amply supplies the funds for an extravagant pre-wedding shopping trip.

The women head out to the chosen stores where they split into shopping teams and spend every last dime on the new bride. The bride will give her input on some of the items, while others are chosen for her as surprises. Being practical is **not** the goal; spoiling, indulging, and spicing things up for the newlywed is!

During these "welcome to the family" scenarios, the point is to send the clear message:

"We love you."

"We enjoy you."

"You are a valued family member."

Enthusiastic acceptance is the signature of a loving family.

Anchor Points

Make Detailed Plans

Make your plans very specific and well in advance of the event. Book your reservations, invite guest speakers, purchase tickets, etc. Leave nothing to chance, except a little breathing room for the spontaneous to occur.

Get dates on the family calendar as soon as possible; a year in advance is not too early. It can be even better having a regularly chosen date, like the first weekend in August each year, when it is a recurring event. Everyone is busy, but will want to be at these gatherings, so give them plenty of notice to work it into their schedules.

Make Visiting your House a Fun Adventure for Kids

Purchase some fun or interesting "toys" that are only available at Grandma and Grandpa's house. We get a lot of mileage out of our four mopeds, and in years past we owned a golf cart the kids were free to drive around in the yard!

Think of age appropriateness with your purchases and consider having different items for the varying ages:

- An antique doll house
- Unique gadgets (usually found in the attic or Grandpa's desk)
- Go cart
- Old adding machine
- Dress up/costume trunk
- Bicycles
- Scooters
- ATV
- Play house

Ideas for Family Gatherings

- Themed Dinner Party
  Invite everyone together for a Hawaiian Luau, a
  Superhero Costume Party, or a Pirate Night including a
  treasure hunt for all ages.

- Game Night
  Some enjoy playing board games or cards, while others
  prefer more interactive games. Some of the best games
  with the most interaction and laughter are ice-breaker
  styled games which can be found on the internet.

- Mystery Weekend
  Make this an annual event and rotate who gets to plan it.
  It works best to have a planning team of two to three
  people. Fill a weekend with fun surprises and allow a lot
  of time for all the family to just be together and interact.
  Decorate for themed meals, go exploring, offer a craft
  project, tour museums, etc. Be sure to save time for
  relaxation and connection time with each other.

- Geocaching
  Geocaching has become a very popular pastime, and it
  can be even more fun when a family does it together; all
  the better if someone takes the lead and sets up a
  personalized hunt for the cache. Plan a route with unique
  treasures which would be particularly fun for your family.
  If you are not familiar with geocaching, just look for it
  online.

- Balloons
  At a family gathering, fill a bouquet of helium balloons
  and place small notes in each one for redeemable prizes
  and booby-prizes. Let everyone chose one balloon and tell
  them each one has a surprise. Ideas:

- o This coupon entitles you to be set free from clean-up duties during this weekend.
- o Take note of who is sitting next to you; for the rest of the weekend, you must make sure there is fresh ice in his or her glass.
- o Cash prize of $10
- o For the rest of the weekend everyone must refer to you as "The Awesome One."
- o You get to take home all the leftover food!
- o You get to choose a grab bag from the prize basket!
- o You get to say, "Me first" one time this weekend. First in the dinner line, first to get dessert, first to whatever you choose and we all will step out of your way!

- **Family Crests**
  Put out a lot of art supplies and ask everyone to design a family crest. Once completed, let everyone explain the parts of their creation and what it means about their family.
- **Write Your Own Fill-in-the-Blank (Mad Lib)®**
  Here is one for a good laugh to wrap up a family weekend. Make up your own, use the one shown on the next page, or find one on the internet. Don't let anyone see the story at first. Ask people to offer the types of words indicated to fill in each blank. Write that word in the blank, even if it doesn't make sense. That is exactly what makes this funny!

Our Family Weekend

We had a perfectly _____ (adjective) time this weekend with our _____ (adjective) family. We stayed at the _____ (adjective) family cabin. The rooms are decorated _____ (adverb) with many stylish _____ (plural noun) that must have cost _____ (number) dollars. In our family, we are all _____ (adjective) conversationalists and _____ (verb) when someone calls out "dinner time!"

_____ (name of person in the room) entertained us with stories of _____ (adjective) _____ (noun).

Grandpa suggested serving _____ (liquid) on the rocks and _____ (name someone in the room) insisted it would be a _____ (adjective) mistake.

Our family isn't very _____ (adjective) but we do boast about having a _____ (grade in school) pursuing work as a(an) _____ (career).

Family weekends are always a _____ (adjective) experience.

Remember, a family worth _____ (verb ending in "ing") for, is a family worth_____ (verb ending in "ing") for. Hope we do it again in _____ (a number) year(s).

Create your own fill in the blank story around the events you have planned or the people involved and everyone will get a good laugh out of it.

Putting the Grand in Grandparent

A Special Calling

Whether it comes as a voice over the phone, accompanied by a hug around the neck, or written in a card, my wife and I delight in the special names bestowed on us when our children first became parents. Grams, Papa-Grandma, Papa, Gramps, Grandma and Grandpa. I'm not sure those titles make me an expert at anything, but they do make me a veteran of a lot of things and an old hand at a few more. At this point in life, I know more about what I really need to appreciate and what just isn't worth the worry.

I know about the importance of listening while another person speaks, and that my way is not the only way to accomplish a task. I know that tenderheartedness wins people over and that young children know whom they can trust. I also know that no matter their age, my family will come around because there is excitement, and stick around because they are loved.

My wife and I enjoy the pursuit of family. This is the chase of a lifetime. It keeps the spice in our marriage and it also has been successful in bonding our family members together, up and down the generations.

Like you, the most significant people in our live are those whom we call family. We want to have many noteworthy encounters where we make memories doing crazy, silly things. Likewise, we want significant encounters where we pass along important family history and the values that carry us through life. It is a special calling to be a grandparent, and I don't want to miss a moment of what this time in life is supposed to be.

Grandparents today face a lot of challenges that were not as prevalent in previous years. Those precious faces in the pictures hanging on the refrigerator door may live across the town, across the country or across the globe. They may only be available for limited visitations because of divorced parents and stepfamilies. Some grandparents feel distant from their grandchildren just because of the technological crevasse that seems to separate the generations. There is still much hope for connecting on a meaningful level with our grandchildren, but we must put some work into a grand plan to make grand things happen.

Ambassador to Your Family

What if you picked up the phone and found the president of the United States was calling to ask you to act as an ambassador to a specific country? This country was in need of improved communication and stewardship, a bridging of culture gaps, and provision of aid and relief. In this position, you could have the potential of changing the history of this country forever. Would you take the job? Of course, you would! How exciting, and what an honor. In effect, this is the calling of a grandparent in the lives of their grandchildren.

Our grandchildren's parents have the responsibility for meeting their children's basic needs, which includes providing guidance and discipline and shaping their lives. Our job as a good ambassador is to back up the parents, and fill in the gaps when it is warranted.

The parents, being the reigning king and queen of this particular country to which you have been called as ambassador, require that all our best intentions be subservient to their wishes. By backing up the parents and respecting their wishes, we continue the shared spirit of "us" working together in this family.

God never intended for parents to retire, so even if your children are now adults with their own children, you still have a supporting role to play in their lives by backing them up as parents.

Whether you are an ambassador, a business executive, or a grandparent, you need to approach the people, and their customs, values and even bizarre traditions with care. Get to know your grandchildren, and do your best to understand their generation and what they value and enjoy. Ask questions and pay attention so that you will find out what they like and dislike. Being a good listener and showing genuine interest in your kids and grandkids creates a foundation for relationship building and cross-generational involvement in each other's lives.

Stepping into the technological realm of this generation can cause serious culture shock for us grandparents. Sadly, I know of many grandparents who have just decided not to make the effort to keep up with cell phones, texting, and social networking via the internet. Many treat it as if it is the mortal enemy of the aging set. At some point, we need to realize that good communication with this generation means we must communicate using their technology.

I have a cell phone with texting and email, because this is how young people connect and I want to be connected with them. I even figured out how to text emoticons. It is pretty easy; ask any teenager and they can show you all kinds of great things on these phones. This has the added benefit of making them feel quite useful as they give you a lesson or two.

Today, I can use the computer to have a personal visit with my granddaughter and her husband in another country, and text grandchildren a quick message so they know I want to see them. I can email and fax important documents to my son, whose office is about ten steps from my own, so you would think I could get out of my seat and carry the message. No, no, I want to be "with it!" I want to embrace this generation's technology. I want to be connected.

If you are a Broadway musical buff, perhaps you may have seen the stage play *Bye Bye Birdie*. If so, you will remember the scene where the curmudgeonly older man stomps across the stage, arms flailing, ranting and singing, *"I don't know what's wrong with these kids today!"* They may do things very differently than our generation, but kids are kids and every generation has had its quirkiness.

Developing inroads with kids means taking the initiative to get things started. Engage them in conversations that show your interest in their lives. Accept and love them just as they are, even with their strange music, unusual hairstyles, weird friends, and odd sayings. They are growing and trying new things, and they need the freedom to be who they are. As long as their quirky ways are not destructive or disrespectful, we need to show them we care most about their heart and the value they bring to the family. Lead by example and share your values. As children grow, they become like those who influenced them most.

Tenderhearted grandparents, who are patient, kind and accepting, find that they have grandchildren who really do want a relationship where they can let down their guard. They appreciate a safe place to share their struggles, fears, frustrations and aspirations: a place where they will not be judged or lectured, and where the conversation will stay in complete confidence. As we

166

develop this sort of bond with our grandchildren, we also create an effective conduit to communicate our values and dreams with them. It is a wonderful thing when we have a strong connection both up and down the generations.

Checklist for the effective Grandparent Ambassador

- Love unconditionally
- Show acceptance of their quirkiness
- Be a good listener and hear what they are saying
- Forgive and ask for forgiveness when needed
- Encourage
- Get to know their likes and dislikes
- Provide for certain needs. Help with homework, purchase a few items which are outside of the family budget, offer a ride someplace, etc.
- Make a plan to spend quality time together

Roll out the Welcome Mat

It never felt like an ordinary day when we would take the kids to visit my parents. I'm not sure if my adult children could even give you an accurate description of the front door of my parent's home, or attest to whether or not it had a door bell. Once my folks heard our car pulling into the driveway, they would throw open the door and hurry out to meet us, with hugs for everyone, smiles and laughter, and the littlest ones scooped up in Dad's arms. My parents' home was a place where love flourished, and they never held back their emotions. In fact, they soared with delight over our visits, showing us in a highly demonstrative manner that our family coming over was a big deal and brought them much joy.

Mom always had little goody bags prepared for each of the kids and Dad always took the time to make plans for a couple of activities while we were there. Maybe it was just a walk to the park or playing games, but he always put some thought into our family time because he understood the importance of giving everyone something to look forward to.

Mom and Dad prepared for the younger children who needed an outlet for their wiggles or creativity, balancing those activities with time for us adults to sit over a cup of coffee and homemade pie. We would talk and connect in a much-needed adult manner. After our visit, Dad would walk us to the car and always stand there talking just a bit more. Soaking up those last moments together was like the last taste of a scrumptious dessert. It made me feel special to have parents who loved our visits and wanted to be with my family right up until we pulled out of the driveway.

I know my dad was just acting from his heart, but I'm sure some modern psychologist could give a detailed analysis of how my dad's physical presence, eye contact, firm hug, and words of encouragement created an atmosphere of love and security for our family. It was just the way he was, and it was just the way my folks loved all of us.

I think it is unfortunate when grandparents don't take the time to plan fun activities for their family when they come to visit. In some cases, it is more like the grandchildren are there to entertain the older generation. Often they do, but we need to keep this going both up and down the generations. If you want your grandchildren to look forward to visits at your home, you need to make sure you have some key ingredients on hand. However you serve it up, those key ingredients need to create fun and security.

Our homes should be welcoming to our grandchildren, and filled with things they can touch and play with, so they feel a sense of belonging, acceptance and intimacy with you. My wife Esther always emphasizes, *"It's not about how perfect your house looks, just make it comfortable and welcoming to everyone."* Esther has the gift of hospitality, and our entire family receives the blessing of her enthusiasm and creativity.

As much as I value my family, I could not pull off some of the crazy ideas we come up with alone. Esther is like an artesian well when it comes to ideas for unique family gatherings and activities. She is a dedicated wife, mother, and grandmother who is enthusiastically on board with this vision of keeping all the generations engaged with one another and growing together. I know I am a lucky man, and recently a few of my grandchildren remarked on this at a family gathering. *"Grandma is the one who is always pulling the details together. She will be working behind the scenes and cooking everything so that Grandpa can go play."*

We are a team, and I give her all the credit she so greatly deserves in sowing enjoyment and strong bonds into our family. It is work!

Stick Around

It's no wonder many families feel a disconnect between the generations. These days, many in the retiree set are looking forward to their new freedom. By following the world culture, they spend their time roaming the countryside in pursuit of sun and new adventures or hobbies. Others find their retirement as a time to volunteer for humanitarian efforts, and many even leave the country to work in areas of the world with very significant needs. These pursuits have value and are actually quite healthy. My wife and I have enjoyed our share of travels and overseas missions trips. They have added a lot of perspective to our lives, and we are glad for the opportunity. A few of these trips have included grandchildren as our co-adventurers. While I think it is healthy to have personal interests, they should not be to the extent that they create distance in the family relationships. Some of these folks may not realize the huge influence for good and for relationship building they are missing out on with their children and grandchildren.

The problem comes when grandparents relocate their lives and become completely absent from the lives of their children and grandchildren, totally missing how much their family needs and wants for them to be around. Your adult children and grandchildren may not communicate it outwardly, because they won't want to step in the way of your happiness, but deep down most of them will feel the disappointment of your absence and their lives are different because of that void. Some families find separation due to work or military deployment to be unavoidable, but to the extent you can control it, stick around! Otherwise you will miss out and so will your family.

Senior communities around the country are desperate for people to come in and visit with the elderly. They will invite school groups and community organizations just to come in and sit with these lonely elderly folks, many of whom are sad because their families rarely come to visit. Why is this? Well, if the grandparents are not making an investment in family relationships with their children and grandchildren earlier in life, there is little motivation for the kids to come around in the later years. It feels wrong and seems heartless, but that is how this scenario is playing out. Here is the tough truth: If we are spending our healthy, empty-nest years chasing our own interests and ditching our family, we should not expect them to be there for us in our twilight years. Simply put, if we show interest in our children and grandchildren when they are young, they will show interest in us when we are old.

Grand Indulgences

A truly *grand* grandparent does not have to be financially wealthy to give their grandchildren a rich inheritance. Like many involved grandparents, I want to invest my time in something that will outlive me, and yes, I want to engage with and even spoil my grandchildren. Appropriate spoiling of grandchildren is allowed in anyone's book. We spoil our grandchildren by indulging them with our time, attention, and the extras of life which may not be available at home due to tight family budgets.

It energizes the kids with hope for our relationship when they see us grandparents as people who still have gusto, ideas and exuberance for life. We have enjoyed camping trips, sleepovers, storytelling, trips to unique or special places, themed dinner parties, holiday celebrations and more. Some of the sweetest memories are so simple, but you have to be there to experience them. You have to be there to get to be the big person with the extra-long arms that can reach the cookies. You are also the heroic person who is not afraid to tell Mom and Dad that one more cookie is okay.

Grand Accomplice

While the other adults were busy chattering and playing a game, one of my granddaughters chose me as her co-conspirator for a very important mission. Her chubby little fingers pressed into my cheeks to the point that I must have looked like a fish with lips pursed. "Grandpa, will you get me a cookie?" she whispered looking over her shoulder, making sure we were far enough away from enemy lines. Her mother had turned her down for another cookie some time ago, but I was clearly being invited into a secret mission and had a very important role to play. Maintaining her hold on my cheeks she slowly leaned her forehead against mine so that we were eye to eye for complete understanding. "The pink one," she said slowly and directly, almost mouthing the words. No doubt, I knew my role and had been commissioned by a mastermind from the cookie commandeer corps. With one subtle movement, I obtained the cache, and we made a timely exit to enjoy the bounty together.

Grinning from ear to ear, this little angel was enjoying the victory in the arms of her hero: me!

One of the greatest forces in bonding between grandparents and their grandchildren is the fact that we share a common enemy, *the parent!* Parents are obliged to make responsible decisions and enforce rules and boundaries, which are all so dreary to the grandchildren and grandparents who just want to nab the moment. Small indulgences are one of the sacred and untouchable privileges of grandparents, but they must never interfere with the ultimate wishes of the parents. Always demonstrate to the child that you and their parents are a team with their best interest at heart. Otherwise, you could be setting the family up for serious friction and relational damage. With simple spoiling, the parent will usually smile or pretend to scold the naughty grandparent, but if they ever seriously disapprove, we must back them up 100 percent.

I remember my own grandfather allowing me to dunk my cookie in his coffee when we thought no one else was looking. Unceremoniously, I would plunge my cookie into his cup of steaming coffee and chomp away, enjoying the lingering flavor and the knowledge that grandpa and I shared this ritual together. A simple act of indulgence is one avenue to forging a relationship with a young person. It will pay off in dividends down the road when that young child becomes a teenager or young adult who looks to you for advice or to be a listening ear.

Babysitting

My daughter Kathy, reminiscing about my parents:
"As children we were so fortunate to have the grandparents we had. I remember that Grandpa had keys to the zoo because he was the director of

the Point Defiance Park greenhouses and often went in, after hours, to take care of the plants. Sometimes we got to go with him, and to this day I remember lying in bed at their house at night, which was very close to the zoo, and hearing the sound of the lions roaring. We all loved staying at their house on the weekend, because every Saturday night was bath time, followed by chocolate milkshakes, and then we watched the Lawrence Welk show. Then it was off to bed, because the next morning they always took us to church and included us in everything they did."

I could never trump my dad as a grandparent. Let's face it, he had the keys to the zoo and that makes him a hero to my kids! I love the thought of my dad holding this prized place in my children's memories.

I owe a debt of gratitude to my parents for all the times they kept the kids so Velda and I could get away for some much needed "us" time. The greatest part of the gift was that we always had peace of mind when we left the children in their care. We knew they would be well taken care of, and we also knew how much the kids loved being with their grandparents. To this day, they talk about the goody bags Mom always had waiting for them and the games Dad would play with them on the floor. All of our children developed deep bonds and personal relationships with my parents that were absolutely golden. I have to say, during those busy years, it certainly was a blessing to our marriage to be able to get away from time to time.

Now, Esther and I are not only grandparents, but we are great-grandparents as well, and have no plans of slowing down in all the ways we can be involved in these young lives. We enjoy time with these young ones and want them always to feel welcome and loved in our home.

Esther often says, "I love it when the great-grandkids come over and we get to babysit. It also gives me a chance to talk with their parents [our adult grandchildren] when they are dropping off and picking up, so it is real good all the way around."

Babysitting the grandchildren is never a chore or a burden. No, it's more like adventure night filled with snuggle time, story books, roasting marshmallows, and drinking hot chocolate with whipped cream piled so high it touches their noses. We enjoy camping in a tent in the living room and sharing stories: the great stories that only grandparents can tell because we have been around for a long, long time and know lots of stories. The grandchildren always love to hear stories about the things their parents did as children. Even more, they like to hear stories from the good old days when we were youngsters.

We have been fortunate. Our children and adult grandchildren are always very respectful of our time and obligations, and are careful not to overload us with babysitting the kids to the point that it loses the fun both for the children and for us.

The word "grandparent" is a noun, something like a statue, but grandparent*ing* is a verb and puts this special calling into action. Any grandparent who jumps into this role knows what an immense source of joy it is to be involved in their grandchildren's lives. Babysitting is the perfect opportunity to be close with the younger generation, and it is fuel to keep us young at the same time.

Going Up?

"Good evening Sir, Madame, you look ravishing this evening. Going up? Ninth floor, fine dining and an evening of distinction for high school prom night."

Dressed in my tuxedo, as close to a New York elevator operator as I could be, I was the man to greet all the young guests and run the elevator for our grandson's senior prom dinner. Earlier in the week his mom, Cheryl, had called my wife and explained their plan to transform the top floor of an old empty building into an elegant dining experience for her son Nelson and his friends on the evening of their prom. She asked us to play a key role to bring this evening together, and we were delighted to be included.

We arrived early to help with the decorating, served food, greeted guests, and I even acted as an unassuming butler once the evening was underway. The fact that the event was over a two-hour drive away did not slow us down a bit. Sure, I'll stand in as the elevator operator, decked out in a tuxedo with shined shoes, a swagger, and smooth repartee. We loved being a part of this night, and we loved that our daughter knew she could call on short notice and, if at all possible, we would be there. That's how we do it. If we can be there, you can bet we will.

Being available to your family and simply being present in their lives conveys an undeniable message of the value you see in them. Absence does not always make the heart grow fonder. Absence will place a big question mark in the minds of others about how interested we are in growing the relationship. It isn't that we intrude on every detail of our children's and grandchildren's lives. That would be equally unhealthy. We just make sure there is a dependable attitude and rhythm around family involvement.

GKW
Est. 2007

Not Just a Weekend. It's a Way of Life! Unpredictable, Unforgettable, Unfiltered. Those are the words our adult grandchildren had printed on T-shirts for everyone at our last Grandkid Weekend. Bull's eye, I say! That is exactly how we hope they view this weekend.

Typically, the grandkids arrive on Friday evening for a weekend designed just for them. We toss all the room keys into a big bowl and have them draw out a key. Since not all accommodations are created equal, we think this is a fair and fun way to determine who sleeps where. My wife will often place family pictures of past gatherings next to a goody bag or gift basket in each room. What a treat for each one to find! (Since Esther is an ace at shopping year round for these things, we never feel too stretched in our budget when pulling it all together.) After everyone has settled in and had some time to reconnect, we kick off our first caper.

One time we passed a bowl of jelly beans around the room, and told everyone to choose their favorite color, but not to eat it yet. Once chosen, we told them, "These are your teammates. All the red jelly bean people over here, greens go over there," and so on. "Now get with your team and jump in someone's car. Then follow us, and we will explain once we get to our next location."

The grandkids are very spontaneous and always play along with our crazy ideas. On this occasion, they followed us across town to a couple thrift stores. At the door of the store, we handed each one a five-dollar bill and said you have fifteen minutes to go in and find everything you need for tonight's costume dinner party. We told one group they were to find cowboy costumes, another group were superheroes, and the last group were to dress as hillbillies. Ready, set, go!

Running through the aisles, the teams tossed shirts, belts and hats back and forth while rummaging through piles of cast-off finery. "Here, try this!" Or, "You'll need this hat!" The most outrageous costume was donned by our grandson, who everyone is more accustomed to seeing in military or professional attire. He showed quite the fashion flair in his gold spandex superhero attire. In the way only laughter and silliness can, this evening's activity was just the ice-breaker we needed to set the stage for a relaxed and successful weekend.

These winsome activities create an atmosphere where it is easy to let down your hair and draw closer to the family you are with. While we never want our family to feel unnecessary pressure when they are unable to attend any of these gatherings, we do want for them to be able to count on a certain amount of family tradition. Grandparents are often the keepers of long-held and favored traditions. When we are all together, laughing and talking about the years gone by warms the hearts of everyone.

Here are a few of our favorite traditions:

Grandkid Mystery Weekend

This is a weekend just for our older career-aged and married grandchildren. We provide a comfortable place for them to stay, lots of good food and beverages, with numerous fun activities and chances for all these cousins to keep close relationships. Each year the activities are different, and we keep them a surprise just to heighten the anticipation over what's to come. Here are some of our favorite activities.

- Hay rides
- Costume theme dinners (pirate, luau, western, superhero, etc.)
- Inspiring and motivating speakers
- Trophy for the person with the best story about something really "dumb" that happened in their life this past year.
- Geocaching (our own locations and cache)
- Goofy bowling
- Skating
- Dinner cruise
- Boat parade
- Evening talk time around the fire with snacks

We set the date for this weekend a year in advance, and all the grandkids look forward to attending. One year we sent out a questionnaire asking for their input. One question was whether we should skip this gathering for a while, or change to every other year. The voters were heard, and we continue this as an annual event.

Individual Time with Younger Grandkids

Individual time with the younger ones has been a focus of ours so that we get to know their unique personalities. It doesn't matter how much money you spend, so just keep to your comfortable budget. We have often taken grandchildren camping and boating, but if you can set the money aside, a larger trip can be a grand memory maker.

Long Distance Grandparents

Unfortunately, nobody gets a practice run at raising a family. This is a one-shot, give-it-your-all kind of deal. Like most grandparents, my wife and I have given our best to this wonderful season in life. However, if there is one thing I would have done differently as a grandparent, it definitely would be working harder at the amount of time I spent with grandchildren who live out of town. Distance is a challenge for many grandparents, and without a good effort to reach those kids, the relationship will become a little limp.

I should have made the drive more often, stuck more notes in the mail, picked up the phone a few more times. As it is, we have good relationships with our out-of-town grandkids, and they know we would do anything we could for them, but those extra moments sure would be sweet to hold onto now.

178

Anchor Points

Relax and Let Your Grandchildren Play with Your Stuff
Having things for the grandchildren to do at your house is important. Let them have fun at your house and use your stuff.

Let them bake in the kitchen, investigate the attic, look through photo albums, play with old adding machines, record players, and the like.

Have special toys and gear that may only be found at Grandma and Grandpa's house :

- Antique doll house
- Old golf cart
- Bicycles
- Mopeds
- Yard games like bocce ball, badminton, or croquet
- Craft supplies
- Library of books that are interesting to children
- Fishing gear
- A nice tea set that is available for play
- Old family movies, converted to a format that is easy to play
- Trunk full of dress-up clothes and costumes
- Art easel with paints and canvas or poster board

Pray
It is vital that we pray for our children, grandchildren and their future spouses.

Encourage Reading
Parents and grandparents should make a practice of regularly giving good books to their children and grandchildren. The person your child or grandchild will become is dependent upon the people they associate with and the books they read.

Grandma and Grandpa's Reading Incentive
Set up your own reading incentive program for your grandchildren. It could be a summer plan or a year-round event. Here are some suggested themes:
- Heroes
  Read four books about different heroes. This could be books about people with a great story who have sacrificed and made a difference in the world.
- Map It
  Put up a map of the United States and invite your grandchildren to read a book from each state. It could be about that state, or a famous person from that state, or the author may be from that state. Once the book is finished, place a marker of some sort on the state to mark it off for the grandchild. Once all 50 states have been covered, have a big Americana celebration or offer a prize. Maybe take a road trip to see some of America's most interesting sights.
- Eras
  Make this a family-wide reading event. Establish the different decades or eras for the books to be selected from and make a chart to fill in once the books have been read. Offer a special party where everyone dresses in the era of their favorite book and have everyone tell a little about their book.

- "I Can Read" Party
  Make it a family tradition that when a youngster first learns to read, Grandma and Grandpa throw an "I Can Read Party." Make a big deal out of reading. Display some of the child's favorite books, decorate and have cake and punch to celebrate. Give the child a chance to read a bit of a favorite book for everyone to hear.
- Book Club
  Invite family members to join a book club. Offer one for youngsters where you read the books out loud to them, and another for teens or adults. Offer books that would interest them in their stages of life, but always make sure they are filled with quality and character-building themes.

Meet the Grandparents

Get to know your grandchildren's other grandparents. Build a relationship as co-grandparents and never rival them in any way.

Control the Tongue

Never speak ill of any family member, especially undermining another adult.

Engage in Meaningful Conversation

These questions are meant to build the relationship by showing genuine interest in the other person and getting to know their personality, values, and interests. Questions should be posed in such a way as to put the grandchild at ease and to create more conversation. It is counterproductive if you allow your thoughts or opinions to make the grandchild feel judged or inadequate in any way. If you don't like the responses you hear, just keep asking more probing questions, and eventually you will get the chance to share your values.

Remember the best answers to questions are two more questions. Keep the conversation stimulating and show your interest.

Conversations with younger grandchildren:
- What was the best part of your week/day?
- What was the worst part of your week/day?
- How is school going?
- What is your favorite subject? Least favorite subject?
- Do you have a lot of homework?
- What do you and your friends like to do during lunch or after school?
- What kind of music do you like to listen to?
- Is there a pet you would like to have?
- Is there something you would like to learn to do?
- What books have you read lately?
- What do you think is the toughest job in the world?
- What would you like to do when you grow up?
- Ask about sports, music, art, drama, or club involvement. Offer an interesting bit of information that maybe you read about some place that is related to one of their interests.

Conversations with older grandchildren:
- What are your plans for work, education, vacation?
- What is your opinion on. . . ? (current events, trends, etc.)
- What is your definition of success?
- What would be the ideal vacation for you?
- What do you value about our family? What would you like to see our family do differently?
- Is there anything you have always wanted to learn to do?

- Which invention or innovation do you appreciate the most in your lifetime?
- What would be a perfect day for you?
- What is the greatest factor that affects most of your decisions? (Family, peers, morals, ethics, spirituality)
- Who do you think is a good role model for your generation?
- What are your thoughts on college?
- Have your read any good books and seen any good movies lately?
- Where do you want to be in five years?
- If married, ask about their spouse's family. Always be encouraging, never questioning or condemning.

Consider How You Will Be Remembered

If you wholeheartedly embrace and incorporate the ideas in this book into your personal existence, you will be remembered as someone with gusto! Leave a legacy worth replicating.

Live Passionately!

Don't be a person who sits and waits for life to come to you. Go out there and grab hold of it. Try new things, live big and love bigger. You set the example of what it is to live a fully engaged life in the view of your family.

Build Others Up

Every day, ask the question, "What can I do to encourage my spouse, my kids, my grandkids, my friends?" Find specific answers to this question. Be a people-builder who sees the good in others and speaks of it.

Consider the Bigger Picture
Just let go of the small stuff because it probably really doesn't matter. Keep your focus on the end goal of building a strong family.

Celebrate!
Find reasons to celebrate and unique ways of doing it. Be the family that throws the homecoming parties for family members who have been away, or have a vintage party to celebrate the anniversary of the ancestors who migrated to America. Viva la family!

Love Lavishly
Believe it or not, some people really struggle with loving unconditionally and without putting up walls. We have nothing to lose when we refine the art of loving our family.

Strive to be a Person of Respect and Honor
W. Clement Stone said, "Do the right thing because it is right." Preserve your reputation and lasting name by living an honest life full of integrity. Future generations will not remember you for your material possessions. They will remember if you were a person of honor, self-sacrifice, nobility, and generosity. If you find a wrong or an injustice, do all you can to right it. You will be remembered for your strength of character.

Give Generously
Give of your time, your money, your service. A life defined by generosity will be remembered for generations.

Allow People to Really Know You

Let your spouse, children and grandchildren know what you value, what you stand for, and who you really are. People who build walls around themselves or remove themselves from family gatherings miss out. Talk openly, tell stories, and engage with your family.

Build a Family Legacy, Not Your Own Legacy

People who value their family above achievements and honors will be remembered for generations. We don't celebrate the wealth they acquired, their travels or their beauty. Collectively, we realize those things don't matter. Building a strong family will carry the greatest honor.

A good character is the best tombstone. Those who loved you,
and were helped by you, will remember you.
So carve your name on hearts and not on marble.
~ C.H. Spurgeon

A family in harmony will prosper in everything.
~ Chinese Proverb

Notes

Notes

Notes

Notes

About Phil Harmon

Family legacy is very important to me. When friends suggested I write this book about the ideas we have used with our family, I decided it might be time to take them seriously and give this a shot. I knew something was going right and wanted to share our values along with the fun, excitement, and some struggles of a committed family life. Coming from a family that enjoys spending time together across the generations, and has not experienced divorce in seven generations, is unfortunately uncommon in our society, but this is the unique truth of our family.

Now, I am at a point in life to benefit from seeing these values and habits lived out in the generations behind me. Recently, my youngest daughter took me out on a "Dad Day." She arranged for a flight museum tour, plenty of talk time in the car, and a delightful dinner in a water front restaurant, all just to stay connected with quality time together.

Leadership and communication skills carry over between business and family life. These skills have value in all types of relationships and have been honed in me though the businesses I have owned over 36 years. Affiliations with various groups like Million Dollar Roundtable, Rotary, and Toastmasters; serving on non-profit boards, such as George Fox University, Barclay College, and In Focus Ministry, has kept me engaged with my community and connected with quality role models to introduce to my family.

Motivational speaking is a passion of mine and I have spoken at events for national insurance companies, non-profits and other organizations on various ministry and business subjects.

For information about this book, to chat about life, or to arrange speaking engagements please contact me by email at *peh42@comcast.net* or call me at (360) 391-3711.

About Jacqueline Rae

I never quite know the magic moment when a friendship begins, but about 14 years ago the Harmon family entered my life and took my understanding of friendship, mentoring, and family life to a whole different level. When I was asked to write this book with Phil, I jumped at the opportunity because I had watched their family dynamic for years and wanted to become a student of the way they purposefully and fully experience family life. The Harmon's have been very supportive of my family and have stood by our sides, and I know there will be many more time that my husband and I will seek their guidance as we grow in our own family leadership and spirit. Our goal in writing this book was to fill each page with so many pearls of wisdom and practical application that the reader wouldn't just read this book once, but would return to it again and again for fresh ideas.

Leadership and mentoring are both very important to me, and I have used writing and speaking as outlets for both. Nothing pleases me more than to share my faith and values through, honest talk, storytelling, laughter and encouragement. As a resident of the Skagit Valley, I enjoy all the Pacific Northwest has to offer in hiking, biking and kayaking. Setting out on an adventure with my husband of twenty-four years and our two sons is my greatest delight.

For speaking engagements and book promotion, contact Jacqueline at *liveforjoy@vlscott.com*.

Ready or not, here life comes!

Bring us to your event or Facebook conversation

Phil Harmon and Jacqueline Rae are both lively storytellers who offer straight talk on the topic of parenting and its lifelong commitment. Encouraging and equipping parents through the good, the bad, and the ugly of family life, these two will have you laughing in one moment and focused on your purpose in the next.

Invite us to your event

- Parenting seminars
- Couples retreats
- Civic organization events
- Club events

Contact us at *liveforjoy@vlscott.com* or through our Facebook page, Parenting Lasts a Lifetime.

Tag us on Facebook

Include us in a conversation about any of the aspects of *Parenting Lasts a Lifetime* and we will join the conversation.